ESSAYS ON LITERATURE

ESSAYS ON LITERATURE

BY

EDWARD CAIRD, LL.D., D.C.L.

LATE MASTER OF BALLIOL COLLEGE, OXFORD

KENNIKAT PRESS, INC./PORT WASHINGTON, N. Y.

ESSAYS ON LITERATURE

First Published 1892
Reissued 1968 by Kennikat Press

Library of Congress Catalog Card No: 68-8224
Manufactured in the United States of America

CONTENTS

DANTE IN HIS RELATION TO THE THEOLOGY AND ETHICS OF THE MIDDLE AGES

DANTE as the Interpreter of Mediæval Catholicism—
Relation of his Poetic Form to his Matter—His Effort
after Poetic Realism—Is the *Commedia* an Allegory?—
Why Dante's Theme is the Other World—How Christianity became a Religion of the Other World—Three
forms of the Mediæval Dualism in Dante. (1) *Opposition
of this to the Other World*—Contrast of Other Religions
with Christianity—How Dante makes the Other World
an Idealisation of this World—The *Inferno* as a Descend-
ing Scale of Vices—The *Purgatorio* as an Ascending Scale
of Atonement—The *Paradiso* as an Ascending Scale of
Beatitude. (2) *Opposition of Empire and Church*—Its Connection with the Opposition of Philosophy and Theology
—Virgil and Beatrice—Dante's Hope of a Reforming
Emperor—His Attack on the Popes—The "Grand
Renunciation"—Criticism of his Political Dualism. (3)
Opposition of the Natural and the Spiritual—The Ethical
and the Theological Virtues—Union of Earthly and
Heavenly Love in Beatrice—Relation of the Contem-
plative and the Active Life—Religion and Morality—
Dante's Poem as the Euthanasia of Mediæval Dualism.

THE opinions of Dante, like those of every great writer who has treated of ethical, political, or religious subjects, have been made the battle-ground of bitter controversy. Apart from those who fall into the shallow trap of seeking the greatness of the poet in some secret doctrine which can be read by the aid of a verbal key, there are many who have sought for Protestantism, and some who have sought for Socialism, or even Nihilism, in his pages.[1] Their interpretations, as was to be expected, have called out those of an opposite school, who have turned him into a champion of orthodoxy, and have treated his denunciation of the Papal policy as a separable accident of his poetry.

Now in a sense it may be maintained, that both parties are " right in what they affirm and wrong in what they deny." Those who see in Dante's words the germs of religious and political change are not altogether in error, though they sometimes

[1] E. Aroux : *Dante Hérétique, Révolutionaire, et Socialiste.*

look for the evidence of their view in the wrong place. For the writers who are most revolutionary in their ultimate effect are not those who violently break away from the institutions of the past and set up a new principle against them, but rather those who so thoroughly enter into the spirit of those institutions that they make them, so to speak, transparent. When the soul becomes visible, the body is ready to drop away. We often find systems of doctrine surviving the most violent attack from without, and apparently only deriving new vigour from the contest. But one thing there is which they cannot survive—viz., being thoroughly understood and appreciated ; for the intelligence that has fully appreciated them has *ipso facto* grown out of them and beyond them. It has extracted the principle from its former embodiment, and so made it capable of entering into combination with other principles to produce new forms of life and thought.

It is in this relation that Dante stands to mediæval Catholicism. In attempting to revivify its ideas, he " betrayed its secret." As Plato in his *Republic* developed the ruling ideas of Greek politics to a point at which they necessarily break through the form of the Greek state and destroy it, so Dante, in giving a final and conclusive utterance to mediæval ideas, at once revealed the vital source of their power, and showed where they come into contradiction with themselves and point beyond themselves for their completion. The attempts made to prove that Dante was a " Reformer before the Reformation," or a " Revolutionary before the Revolution " are, in the sense in which they were made, vain and futile : and, in spite of the rough way in which he denounces the state of things ecclesiastical and political, writers like Ozanam and Hettinger have no difficulty in showing Dante's complete orthodoxy, and his complete acceptance of the Catholic system of life and thought. Even from the first the Catholic Church recognised that the attacks of Dante were the wounds of a friend, and that it would be an absurdity to put in the *Index* a poem which was the most eloquent of all expressions of its own essential ideas. The revolutionary power of Dante's poetry lay in quite a different direction. It lay just in this, that Dante held up to mediæval Catholicism its own ideal, the very principle on which it rested and from which it drew all its power, that he judged it by that ideal, and that by that ideal he found it wanting. For, although, as " the most hopeful son of the Church Militant," Dante seemed to himself to be able to indicate one simple way in which the old order of Church and State could be restored, to all but himself the very expression of the conditions

necessary for this return to the past was the demonstration of its impossibility.

In this essay, it is not proposed to consider
Dante as a poet, or at least to enter into any questions directly connected with the poetic form in
which he has expressed himself, but rather to treat
him as a writer who sought in his own way to read
the signs of his times, and to declare to others the
lesson he had thus learnt.

In doing so, we are judging Dante according to a
standard which he himself has set up. The poetic
form, indeed, is inseparable from Dante's thought,
as is shown by his comparative failure to utter himself in prose ; but to himself it was, so to speak, an
inseparable accident, necessary only as the vehicle
of his message to his time, as the form through
which alone he could express his whole conception
of human life, and " justify the ways of God to
man." If ever there has been a poetry which was
indifferent to its own matter, it was certainly not
the " sacred poem to which heaven and earth had
set their hands so that for many years it had made
the poet lean." The *Divina Commedia* was for
Dante simply the last perfect expression of the
same thought, which in all his other works, both of
prose and verse, it had been his effort to utter. It
is not, indeed, a didactic poem in the ordinary
sense of the word. Dante was too perfect an artist

not to see that the direct practical movement of the preacher or the orator is alien to the contemplative spirit of poetry. But it is didactic in the sense that it is an effort to exhibit the ideal truth of things, the moral law of the world, which is hidden from us by the confusion of phenomena, and the illusion of our own passions. Hence the first problem suggested by the *Commedia* is, how Dante's poetry becomes the vehicle of a complete philosophical and theological view of human life without ceasing to be poetry.

We may answer, in the first place, that the reason why Dante is able to be philosophical without ceasing to be poetical, is the same which enables Plato to approach so closely to poetry without ceasing to be a philosopher. By Dante, as by Plato, every part is seen in the light of the whole, and therefore becomes a kind of individual whole in itself. Dante can be faithful to truth without ceasing to be a poet, because for him the highest truth is poetical. His unceasing effort to reach the poetry of truth and the truth of poetry may be evidenced in many ways.

He began his career as a poet by a kind of Wordsworthian reaction against the affectations of the Provençal school, from which he received his first lessons in the art of verse. In a well-known passage in the *Purgatorio*, Bonagiunta di Lucca,

one of his poetical predecessors, questions him as
to the reason of the superiority of his lyrics.
Dante answers that his secret was simply strict
adherence to the truth of feeling. " I am one,
who, when love inspires me, make careful note of
what he says, and in the very manner in which
he speaks within, I set myself to utter it." Bonagiunta is made to answer: " Now, I see the
obstacle which made me and the Notary and Guit-
tone fall short of the sweet new style, which in
your verses sounds in my ears. I see clearly
that your wings follow closely after the dicta-
tion of love, which was certainly not the case with
us."

In the description of outward things, Dante's
minute accuracy, as of one who wrote always "with
his eye on the object," is one of his most obvious
characteristics. Sometimes he goes so far in breaking through the conventional limitations of poetical
language as to give us a shock of surprise, like
that which we receive from the homely detail of
Wordsworth ; though in Dante we never meet
with those pieces of crude undigested prose to
which Wordsworth sinks in his less inspired
moments. More often Dante falls into this kind
of error in relation to the prose, not of bare fact,
but of thought. In his anxiety to utter the whole
truth of his theme, and to make his work a kind of

compend of philosophy and theology, he sometimes introduces definitions and expositions of doctrine, which are too abstract to be fused into unity with any poetic symbol ; as, for instance, in the curious Aristotelian lecture on the relations of the soul and the body, which he puts into the mouth of the poet Statius.[1] Generally, however, the intractableness of Dante's theme is overcome partly by the Platonic cast of his thoughts, to which we have already referred, and partly by the realising force of imagination with which these thoughts are grasped. The synthetic power of poetry, which individualises all that is universal, is made the servant of the philosophic synthesis, which overcomes abstraction by grasping ideas in their relations. The passage in the thirteenth canto of the *Paradiso*, where St. Thomas is made to expound the scale of being, and the parallel passage in the first canto, are good instances of the way in which Dante conquers this difficulty. And it is remarkable that he succeeds, not by expansion, but by compression of thought ; in other words, he makes the conceptions of philosophy and theology poetic, not by diluting them in metaphors, but by a concentrated intensity of expression, which suggests the connection of each part with the whole, and the presence of the whole in every part.

[1] *Purgatorio*, xxv.

What, then, is Dante's theme? To this Dante himself gives an answer which might at first sight seem inconsistent with the very nature of poetry, as a direct sensuous presentment of its object. In his letter to Can Grande della Scala, to whom he dedicates the *Paradiso*, he declares that the subject of the *Commedia*, taken literally, is the state of souls after death. But he goes on to say that if the work be taken allegorically, its subject is man, as by the good or ill use of his freedom he becomes worthy of reward or punishment.

Now, many modern critics might be disposed to say that to play in this way with double meanings is necessarily to lose the immediate appeal of poetry to our inner perception, and to " sickly o'er the native hues " of imagination " with a pale cast of thought." Nor can we escape the force of this objection by saying that the allegory is an after-thought, which occurred to Dante only when his poem was completed, and did not affect him during its composition. On the contrary, during the course of the poem he frequently directs our attention to the " subtle veil " under which he half conceals and half reveals a higher truth : and this deeper meaning is suggested to us not only by the numerous symbolic figures which are introduced at each stage of our progress, but by the main lines of the structure of the *Commedia*. Even this might be regarded by some as a concession which was forced upon Dante by the ideas of his time. But, when we look more closely, we see that such a double meaning is no mere literary convention, but that it is inwrought into the very essence of Dante's work. It was, in fact, the necessary condition which he had to fulfil, in order to be, what Carlyle calls him, " the spokesman of ten silent centuries." If Dante was to give poetic expression to the consciousness of the Middle Ages, it was as necessary for him to live in two worlds at once as for Homer to live in one. What characterised the Homeric age was its fresh sense of the reality of life and its interests ; hence the poet of the *Iliad* and the *Odyssey* could introduce the world of the dead only as a shadowy and spectral existence at the extreme verge of his picture of the living world. But to the highest consciousness of the Middle Ages it might almost be said that the parts were inverted, and that the world of the living was but a shadowy appearance, through which the eternal realities of another world were continually betraying themselves. The poet who made himself the interpreter of such a time was obliged to encounter all the difficulties of this strange division of man's being. He must draw his picture, as it were, on windows lightened by an unseen sun. However alien it might seem to the nature of

poetry, or at least to the ordinary theory of its
nature, he had to live in an atmosphere of double
meanings, of crosslights and symbolic references,
in which nothing was taken for simply itself ; and
yet, in spite of this, he had to be " simple,
sensuous, and passionate," in order to be a poet
at all.

It is his strange success in this apparently
impossible task that gives the unique character
to Dante's achievement.   His poem seems as if it
were constructed to refute all the ordinary canons
of poetic criticism, and to prove that genius is its
own law.   But the key to the difficulty is not very
hard to discover.   It is just through the symbolic
nature of his theme that Dante finds his way back
to poetic truth and reality.   It is because the other
world, as he fixes his eyes upon it, turns for him
into an enlarged and idealised counterpart of this
world, because its eternal kingdoms of " Hell,"
" Purgatory," and " Paradise," are for him the
symbol of the powers which underlie and control
the confusing struggle of human life, that Dante
is able to give to his journey through all these
supernatural kingdoms the vivid force of natural
realisation.   Hence it may fairly be said, that
it is just because the *Commedia* is symbolic
that it is true.   Accepting the dualism of the
Middle Age, Dante can transcend it only by

the double reflection of each world upon the other.

The meaning of this last statement will become clearer, if we consider for a moment the nature and origin of that dualism. It arose out of the opposition of Christianity to the ancient forms of life which it had to overcome. As in every great revolution by which a new principle of life has been introduced into human history, it was to be expected that the negative side of Christianity should be the first to manifest itself. Till the enemy was conquered, it was impossible that he should be recognised as not altogether an enemy. The materialism and sensualism, which were partly consequences of the fact that ancient civilisation was in process of decay, made it all but impossible for the Christian, under the fresh inspiration of the most idealistic faith which the world had ever seen, to admit any kindred between the new life and the old. The Church was necessarily militant against the world, till the world was subdued. Only after the first shock of antagonism had ceased, and the new society was secure in itself, did it become possible for it to see that there were many elements in the old system which might be appropriated by it, and used as materials for the new social structure. And it was not till centuries had passed, not indeed till the present age, that it could be discerned that there is a deeper root of unity, from which all religions and civilisations spring, and in view of which even such a change as the introduction of Christianity must be regarded as a step in the development of one life.

Christianity was, therefore, at the outset, and in the eyes both of those who accepted and of those who rejected it, a revolutionary idealism, which, as it turned the cross into the highest symbol of honour, seemed to invert all the old standards of excellence, and all the old criteria of truth. " Those who have turned the world upside down are come hither also."

The characteristic of the new religion, which was most prominent in the minds of its earliest converts, is the antithetic abruptness of its inversion of the outward, and, we may even say, of the inward order of ancient life ; and it was the apparent lawlessness involved in this revolution which turned the prejudice of the world against it. " He hath put down the mighty from their seats, and hath exalted the humble and meek," is the birth song of the new creed ; and St. Paul, who made the first steps toward turning the immediate utterance of Christian feeling into a theory, is continually insisting on the theme that " God hath chosen the weak things of the world to confound the mighty."

The same thing seen from the outside made the Roman emperors regard Christianity as the most fatal and horrible of superstitions, a superstition which inspired the dregs of society with a subversive madness, and made them for the first time unsubmissive to the firm hand of Roman discipline. It is true that Christianity was not outwardly revolutionary in its immediate aims. It preached submission to lawful authority, and not revolt ; and it recognised even the empire that persecuted it as, in a sense, " ordained of God." But the instinct of its enemies was true. It submitted, not because it accepted the world's law, but because it stood so far off from that law that it could easily avoid any conflict with it : because, in the idealism of its faith, it could treat the whole order of secular life as something extraneous and indifferent. The Christian slave endured his chains, because slavery and mastery, the dunghill or the throne, could matter little or nothing to one whose citizenship was in heaven. Such a doctrine hid its revolutionary power in the excess of its spiritualism. But the imperial instinct of Rome recognised that such submission was treacherous, and that the political system of the empire must necessarily be destroyed by the development of a principle, which it could neither assimilate nor overcome. The Church steadily grew and increased within the empire, at once using it, and exhausting its energy by the invasive power of its stronger spiritual life, till in the course of time the imperial authority had to choose between extinction and submission.

The intellectual narrowness that hinders men from grasping more than one aspect of a great principle at one time, and even the limitations of human speech, are continually tending to exaggerate relative into absolute opposition, and to reduce unity into identity. And, as in its distinctive maxim, " Die to live," Christianity contained the germ at once of a deeper antagonism, and of a more comprehensive reconciliation, between the different elements of man's nature, than any previous system, it was inevitable that in its development it should sway between the two extreme poles of Manichæan Dualism and a Pantheism in which all difference of good and evil was lost ; though it could not identify itself either with the one or the other without losing its distinctive character.

The necessity of conquering other forms of belief and of contending with the materialism of ancient civilisation tended at first to throw emphasis upon the negative rather than upon the positive aspect of the Christian maxim. And this tendency was seconded by the order of thought in the maxim itself, which involved that self-realisation should be sought through self-sacrifice. The consequence was that the early Church threw all its weight in this direction, and viewed its own life as essentially opposed to that of the kingdoms of this world, which it expected soon to be subverted by the second coming of Christ. It is, however, noticeable that, in its earliest form, Christianity is less hopeless of the world, less dualistic than it afterwards became : even the Millenarian idea being itself a witness that the first Christians saw no incongruity in the idea that this world should be directly turned into the kingdom of God, or in the hope that, without passing through the gate of death, the faithful should have their mortal nature transformed entirely by the power of the new life. The explanation of this lies partly in the fact that the first Christians received the principle of Christianity in its unevolved completeness, before the tendency to emphasise one side of it had gained strength. Still more it lay in the natural confidence of those who first felt the inspiring power of the new faith, and who had not yet learned to estimate the obstacles that stood between the simple acceptance of the Christian principle in its unexplained generality, and the realisation of it in a complete system of life and thought.

In the first intuitive apprehension of a new idea of life everything seems at once to be attained. In

its universality men seem to possess a present
infinity, a principle of unlimited good, which can
be resisted by nothing because it includes everything.   In this sense Hegel speaks of the infinite
value of the unenfolded religious emotion, as it
exists in the breast of the simplest man who has
felt its power.   But, in another point of view, an
idea so apprehended is merely a germ, which as yet
has shown as little of what it contains or of the real
results to which it will grow, as the acorn shows
of the future oak.   In the course of the second
century, when the first fervour of hope and faith
was over, it began to be seen that the perfect
fruition of the Christian ideal could not be grasped
at once.   The immediate hope of a sudden divine
change of the world was lost, and with it, we might
almost say, the hope of a realisation of Christianity
in this world.   The first steps toward the building
up of an organised community of Christians
brought with them a consciousness of the immense
hindrances, inward and outward, which stood in
the way of the realisation of a kingdom of heaven
upon earth.   And, though the idea that human
nature is capable of a complete purification and
regeneration could not be lost without the loss of
Christianity itself, the belief began to prevail that
such completion can be attained only in another
world.

Hence the apparent contradiction that the principle of Christianity comes to be regarded as unrealisable, just at the time when the first steps are taken to realise it.   It is when the Church has begun to establish itself as one of the political powers of the world, that the expectation of a kingdom of God on earth all but disappears, and Christianity becomes decisively an other-world faith—the hope of a victory to be won, and a fruition to be enjoyed, only beyond the grave. In like manner, it is when the Christian idea has ceased to be a simple consciousness of relation to Christ, when it has put itself in relation to the philosophy of the ancient world and begun to develop into a system of doctrine, that the distinction of faith and knowledge begins to be emphasised, and divine things begin to be regarded as altogether beyond the sphere of the understanding of man.

In the New Testament, and especially in the Epistles of St. Paul, the minor note of sadness— which can never be entirely absent from the expression of the Christian consciousness — is sometimes all but lost in the hope of a joy to be revealed in the near future ; and sorrow takes the aspect of a passing shadow, which is soon to disappear from the new heavens and the new earth. But with the apostolic age this confident spirit passes away, and life begins to be regarded as a pilgrimage in a foreign land, in which the Christian has continually to contend with enemies without and within, and no fruition corresponding to his hopes is to be expected. Existence is thus, as it were, projected into a future beyond the grave, and even the Church is conceived not as the kingdom of God realised on earth, but as an ark of refuge, in which man is to be carried through the storms of life to his true fatherland.

It was by the aid of this conception, which practically deferred the realisation of its ideal to another world, that the Church was enabled to retain that ideal, and yet partly to reconcile itself to the conditions of its existence in a society still only half civilised, and organised on principles alien to Christianity. For the division which was thus made between the secular and the sacred, if in one point of view it tended to exalt the Church at the expense of the State, yet supplied an excuse to the former for tolerating in the latter a kind of life that was not in harmony with its own principles. In this way the revolutionary tendencies of Christianity, the demands of its idealistic morality, and its purely spiritual criteria of judgment were retained, and yet made reconcilable with acquiescence in the *status quo*, and even with a conservative alliance with the existing political powers. The kingdoms of this world were allowed to subsist, nay, their authority was consecrated, by a Church which repudiated all their principles of life and government ; and the doctrine that this life is merely a preparation for another enabled Christianity to be used as an anodyne to reconcile men to the injustices under which they were suffering, rather than as a call to change the institutions which caused such evils. On the other hand, the Church, at least in its dedicated orders, in its priests, monks, and nuns, sought to realise within itself that higher life which it refrained from demanding from the world. But even here the same antagonism betrayed itself ; and the three vows of the " religious " life turned Christianity into an ascetic struggle against nature. Yet such asceticism could not be based on the idea (which underlay earlier ascetic systems) that the natural passions or feelings are in themselves evil. Such a Manichæan division, discordant as it was felt to be with the doctrine of a divine humanity, was once for all rejected and refuted by the first great speculative genius of the Western Church, St. Augustine.

It remained that asceticism should be conceived as a stage of transition, and that the object of it should be taken to be, not to root out nature, but only to purify it. Nature must die to itself that

it might live to God, but it could so die without
perishing ; it could rise again to a new spiritual
life without ceasing to be nature. Nay, if the
mediæval saint could believe that nature had so
" died to live," he could even accept its voice as
divine. On this point, however, he was very
difficult to reassure ; he was, indeed, scarcely willing to admit that the spiritual death of nature,
which is the beginning of a higher life, could come
before the natural death of the body. Hence the
highest morality, the morality of the cloister, remained for him negative and ascetic, and, if he
ever regarded it as a preparation for a positive
morality in which impulse and duty should be
made one, it was in a future life only that he
expected such an ideal to be realised. The tender
feminine voice of mediæval piety, its self-repres-
sion and submission to an evil present, its ardent
longing for a glory to be revealed, its self-morti-
fication and renunciation of the world, and its
exultant consciousness that everything it lost
would one day be regained, its combination of
all-levelling love with the resigned acceptance of
a social state in which men were held down and
held asunder by the most fixed class-divisions, were
the natural results of this curious compromise.
Christianity had brought together so many apparently inconsistent elements of thought and feeling,

that in the first instance it was possible for them to be combined only by distributing them between two worlds. But, after all, it was one mind that lived in both : it was one spirit which was thus divorced from itself, and which was at the same time engaged in a continual effort to overcome the division.

Dante comes at the end of the Middle Ages, and, as has already been indicated, it was his work to bring the mediæval spirit to a consciousness of itself and so to carry it beyond itself. He does so, however, not by the rejection of any of its characteristic modes of thought. He does not, like some of his immediate successors, recoil from the one-sided spiritualism of the Middle Ages, and set against it a naturalistic delight in the beauty of the world of sense. Nor does he rise to that higher perception of the spiritual in the natural which has inspired the best modern poetry. He was no Boccaccio or Heine, raising the standard of revolt in the name of mere nature against all that hindered her free development. Nor was he a Shakspere or Goethe who could spiritualise the natural by force of insight into its deeper meaning. But, accepting without a shadow of a doubt or hesitation all the constitutive ideas of mediæval thought and life, he grasped them so firmly and gave them such luminous expression that the spirit in them broke away from the form. The force of imaginative realisation with which he saw and represented the supernaturalism, the other-worldliness, the combined rationalism and mysticism of the Middle Age, already carried in it a new idea of life. In this view we might say that Dante was the last of mediæval and the first of modern writers. To show that this is the case will be the object of the remainder of this essay.

We may best realise this aspect of Dante's poem by regarding it in three different points of view, and by considering how he deals with three contrasts or antagonisms which run through all mediæval thought and life—though, indeed, they may rather be regarded as different aspects of one great antagonism: *first*, with the antagonism between this and the other world ; *secondly*, with the antagonism between the Empire and the Church, with which in Dante's mind is closely connected the opposition between faith and reason, or between theology and philosophy ; and, *finally*, with the antagonism between the natural and the spiritual, or between the morality of self-denial and the morality of self-realisation.

1. It has already been pointed out that mediæval religion tended to regard the world as a sphere in which man is prepared for a better life, but which has no substantial worth in itself. " This is not

our home," " the native land, the *patria* of the soul, is in heaven," " we are pilgrims and sojourners, who seek for a city that hath foundations." In such sayings we find the distinctive note of mediæval piety, the source at once of its weakness and its strength, of its almost fatalistic resignation to suffering, and of its consoling power. The other world is the inheritance of those who have failed in this ; and the sense of failure, the sense that man is utterly powerless in himself, had in this period altogether expelled the joyous self-confidence of ancient virtue.

This change may be traced to many causes. The sufferings of an age of war and oppression, the insecurity of a time when the tribal bonds of barbarous society were being dissolved, and when the unity of modern nations was not yet established, may furnish a partial explanation ; but still more is due to the agonies of fear and remorse, which took the place of the self-confident animalism and rude freedom of the Teutonic races when brought into the presence of the new spiritual light of Christianity, and to the ascetic recoil from all secular interests, which, as we have seen, was the necessary result of the first conflict of Christian ideas with a world they could not yet transform. These causes tended to develop a kind of religion which withdrew man from the interests of the

present, and, as it were, transferred the centre of
gravity of his life beyond the grave. Such a
religion was in essential contrast with the religions
of classical antiquity, which were in the main wor-
ships of a divine principle revealed in the family
and the State.   And it was equally in contrast with
the religion of the Jews, which, if it took men
beyond the present, yet did not lift them out of
this world, but only carried them forward to a
better future for their race.

It has often been felt as a difficulty by modern
students of the history of religion, that ancient
religions dwelt so little on the concerns of another
world ; but it is a difficulty only because the
mediæval stamp has been so strongly impressed on
our minds that, like Kant, we are ready to say that
" without a belief in a future state no religion can
be conceived."   But the inspiring power of religion
for most of the peoples of antiquity lay, mainly at
least, in the view which it led them to take of this
rather than of another world.   Mediæval Christianity, on the other hand, turned the Jewish
aspiration after a better future on earth into a belief
that man's good can be realised, and his happiness
attained, only in heaven.   And, for what was thus
lost in the inspiring power of the consciousness
of a divine purpose realising itself in the present
life of man, it tried to make up by the idea of

the present life as a preparatory discipline for another.

Now, it is easy to see that such a belief is susceptible of many shades of meaning. It is capable of sinking into the coarsest superstition which barters a joy here for a joy of no higher character in the life to come. Yet, even in that case it may be said, that the joys that are not seen, the desires that cannot be gratified here and now, are by that very fact changed and elevated in character ; if for no other reason, at least because a joy not possessed is always idealised by imagination. And it may be further said that even mediæval Christianity, if it caught men at first by sensuous fears and hopes, contained in itself a provision for their gradual idealisation, as the nature of the Christian life became better known. It admitted of a sort of sliding scale of interpretation from the mere superstitious fear of the vengeance of God to the most saintly desire for inward purity. Still, so long as it laid such exclusive emphasis on the idea of another life—which was broken off from this life by a chasm that could not be filled up—so long as its supernatural was not the natural seen in its ideal truth, but, so to speak, another natural world somewhat differently constituted, so long mediæval religion wanted something which, *e.g.*, even Greek religion possessed. The division of the religious from the secular vocation of man was necessarily a source of disharmony in all his existence. It led naturally and almost inevitably to a separation between divine service and that service of God which is only another aspect of the service of man —a separation which turns religion into superstition, and deprives morality of its ideal character.

Now in Dante's great poem the mediæval form of representation is strictly preserved. Human life is viewed as essentially a preparation for another world, whose awful reality throughout overshadows it, and reduces its interests almost into an object of contempt, except when they are viewed in relation to that world. " O, wretched man, do ye not see that we are worms produced only to contain the angelic butterfly, which flies to justice without a covering," is one of many similar utterances ; and in a remarkable passage in the *Paradiso*, where Dante represents himself as looking down upon the earth from the highest heaven, he makes the minuteness of its apparent size a symbol of the littleness of earthly things as seen from the heavenly point of view. Yet, after all, the eternal world which he exhibits to us is just this world seen *sub specie æternitatis*, this world as it is to one who views it in its moral aspect. And, as we see from the letter to Can Grande della Scala already quoted, Dante means it to be so understood. Thus taken, the *Inferno* and the *Paradiso* are simply Evil and Good in the full development of their abstract opposition, and the *Purgatorio* is simply this world, regarded as a scene of moral struggle and purification. Hence, both in the *Inferno* and in the *Paradiso*, Dante attempts to make the woe and the joy as closely as possible the visible expression of character, which finds its doom in being fixed for ever in its characteristic act or attitude ; and in the *Purgatorio* the same sufferings—which in the *Inferno* had been the penal return of the crime upon the criminal—become the purifying pains through which he frees himself from his sin. Or, looking at it in a slightly different point of view, the descent of Dante through the circles of the " Inferno " is an imaginative picture of the process of moral degradation, and his ascent through the Purgatorial mount, together with his upward flight through the Heavens, is the corresponding vision of the process of moral renovation.

It is in accordance with this idea that, in the upper circles of the " Inferno," Dante begins with the sins of passion, of inordinate indulgence in some finite good, with lust, gluttony, avarice, and prodigality, making the punishment in each case a kind of symbol of the crime, or, as has just been said, the return of the crime upon the criminal.

Those who have yielded to lawless desire are blown about in the dark whirlwind. The avaricious and the prodigal are doomed to the endless task of rolling heavy weights backward and forward, each undoing the other's work. Lowest among the sins of passion Dante puts the discontent which wastes its energy in fretting against the limits of earthly satisfaction, and will not look kindly upon the light of day.[1] Those who have been thus morose and sullen in their lives are plunged in the deep mire, where they continually keep up a monotonous complaint. " Sad were we above in the sweet air, which is brightened by the sun, bearing in our hearts a lazy smoke that hid its light from our eyes ; now are we sad in the black mire." In the next circle is punished the sin of heresy, which is for Dante the deliberate acceptance of the principle of evil in place of the principle of good, or, in other words, the denial of that higher idea of life which raises man above the animals. Those who have thus shut their minds to *il ben del intelletto* are prisoned in fiery tombs. Out of this root of evil principle, according to Dante's way of thinking, spring all the sins of malevolence, of hate of God

[1] Cf. Mr. Harris' essay on " The Spiritual Sense of the Divina Commedia," in the American *Journal of Speculative Philosophy*, for October, 1887, which has suggested some of the above remarks.

and man, beginning in violence and ending in deceit and treachery in all its kinds, which, as involving the utmost corruption of man's peculiar gift of reason, are punished in the lowest circles of the " Inferno."

In the *Purgatorio* the principle of good is supposed to have been restored, and therefore suffering has ceased to be penal, and has changed into the purifying pains by which men free themselves from evil.   Hence, though there is nothing here exactly corresponding to the lower circles of the "Inferno," the lowest terraces of the Purgatorial mountain have still to purge away some remaining stains of the baser forms of sin—stains of pride, envy, and anger—which make a man seek his own good in opposition to the good of his neighbours.   In the fourth circle, man's purification from *accidia*—that torpid and relaxed temper of mind which refuses to be stimulated to action either by divine love or by the desire of finite good—prepares the way for his purgation, in the three highest terraces, from sins of passion, sins in which man gives to finite good the love that should be reserved for the infinite.

Finally, the heavenly journey of Dante carries us up through all the finer shades of spiritual excellence, beginning with the devotion that is not yet unswerving in purpose, the love that still clings to the charm of sense, and the practical virtue which is still haunted by the " last infirmity of noble minds," and ending with the passionate faithfulness of crusaders like Dante's ancestor, Cacciaguida, the pure zeal for justice of kings like Godfrey of Jerusalem, and the perfect devotion of monastic sainthood, whether seraphic in love with St. Francis, or cherubic in wisdom with St. Dominic.

In all this Dante holds to the mediæval point of view, in so far as he makes this world altogether secondary and subordinate to the other ; yet he escapes the mediæval dualism by exhibiting the other world as simply the clear revelation of ideal forces which are hidden from us amid the confused phenomena of our earthly existence. In effect, though not in so many words, the postponement of this world to the other comes simply to mean the postponement of appearance to reality, of the outward show and semblance of life to the spiritual powers that are working in and through it. It is, therefore, no mere afterthought when, in his letter to Can Grande, Dante bids us regard the description of the other world as symbolic of the truth about man's life here. We might even, from this point of view, be tempted to regard Dante's representation of the other world as a mere artistic form under which the universal meaning of our present life is conveyed.   For, even if Dante did not mean to say this, his work says it to us.   His poetical handling of the idea of another life tends to remove from it all that is conventional and arbitrary, and to turn it into the appropriate expression of an ever present moral reality.   And, though some elements of the horror and brutality of the mediæval conception of retribution are still retained in harsh discords of the *Inferno*, and some of the childishness, which mingled with the childlike purity of mediæval piety, in the dances and songs of the *Paradiso*, we may, perhaps, compare these things to the unfinished parts of the statues of Michael Angelo, which exhibit the material the artist had to use, and heighten our consciousness of his power by a glimpse of the difficulty with which he was struggling.

2. In mediæval thought the opposition between this and the other world was closely connected with the second opposition to which reference has been made, the opposition between the Empire and the Church, between politics and religion, and also, as Dante holds, between philosophy and theology. In Dante's prose treatise, the *De Monarchia*, we have an argument in regular scholastic form, in which he tries to defend his own reading of the politico-ecclesiastical ideal of the Middle Age, which was expressed in the maxim : " One God,

one Pope, one Emperor." The following quotation gives the substance of Dante's view:

"If man is a mean between the corruptible and the incorruptible, like every other mean, he must have something in him of both extremes. Further, as every nature is constituted in view of some ultimate end, man, who partakes of two natures, must be constituted in view of a twofold end. Two ends, therefore, the ineffable wisdom of Providence has set before his efforts ; to wit, the beatitude of this life, which consists in the exercise of his proper virtue, and which is figured to us by the Terrestrial Paradise ; and the beatitude of eternal life, which consists in the fruition of the divine vision, and which is represented by the Celestial Paradise. To these different beatitudes, as to different results, we can attain only through different means. To the former we attain by the teaching of philosophy, which guides us in the exercise of the moral and intellectual virtues. To the latter we attain by means of those spiritual teachings which transcend human reason, and which guide us in the exercise of the theological virtues—faith, hope, and charity. These ends and the means to them are exhibited to us, on the one hand, by human reason expressing itself in its fulness in the philosophers, and, on the other hand, by the Holy Spirit, which, through the prophets and sacred writers, through the Eternal Son of God, Jesus Christ, and His disciples, has revealed to us a truth which is beyond nature. But, in spite of all these evidences, human passion would inevitably disregard both the earthly and the heavenly end, unless men, like horses, had their brutal

lusts restrained with bit and bridle. Hence there was
needed, in order to bring man securely to his double end,
a double directing power : to wit, the Holy Pontiff, to
guide him, in accordance with Revelation, to eternal life ;
and the Emperor, to direct him to temporal felicity, in
accordance with the precepts of philosophy. And since
none or few, and these only with the utmost difficulty,
could attain to this haven, unless the waves of deceitful
lust were quelled, and the human race enabled to enjoy
the freedom and tranquillity of peace, *this*, above all,
is the aim to which the Curator of the world, who is
called the Roman Prince, should direct all his efforts : to
wit, that in this mortal sphere life may be freely passed
in peace. . . . . It is clear, then, that the authority
of the temporal monarch descends to him without any
medium from the fountain of all authority—that fountain
which, one and simple in its lofty source, flows out into
many channels in the abundance of the divine goodness.
. . . . This, however, is not to be taken as meaning
that the Roman Emperor is in *nothing* subject to the
Roman Pontiff ; for that mortal happiness, of which we
have been speaking, itself has a farther end in the
happiness which is immortal. Let then Cæsar pay such
reverence to Peter as a first-born son owes to his father,
that, illumined by his paternal grace, he may, with
greater virtue, irradiate the whole circle of the world,
over which he is placed by Him alone, who is the ruler
of all things, temporal and spiritual."

The ideas which Dante thus expresses in prose
govern the whole movement of the *Commedia*.

They explain the contrast between the two guides of Dante—Virgil and Beatrice—the former of whom is immediately taken as the representative of philosophy and of the teachings of reason, and indirectly also of the Roman imperial power which Dante regarded as the source of that secular moral discipline by which man is taught the cardinal virtues of the secular life ; while the latter speaks for a theology based on revelation, and maintains the necessity of that discipline in the three theological virtues, which it is the function of the Church to supply.

The great evil of his time, according to Dante, was that these two different functions had been confused, that the Empire and the Church had become rivals instead of complements of each other, and that by this dislocation of the governing power, the whole life of man had been thrown into disorder : " Ye may well see that it is ill guidance that has made the world stray from good, and not any corruption of the nature of man. Rome, that once gave peace to the earth, was wont to have two suns. Now that one has quenched the other, and the sword has joined with the pastoral staff, they must both wander from the path. For, so united, the one fears not the other." [1]

As is manifest from this passage, the main re-

[1] *Purgatorio*, xvi. 103.

sponsibility for the perversion of the divine order of life, lay, in Dante's opinion, with the Church, and especially with the Papacy, which, as he held, had abandoned its proper functions, and had grasped at the imperial authority. For, by this policy, the Papacy alienated its natural ally, and gave opportunity for the undisciplined licence of the communes and the sanguinary ambition of France, to which the Papacy itself ere long became a victim. And the main cure for this state of things which Dante requires and prophesies is, that some great emperor or servant of the empire, some Henry VII. or Can Grande, should appear to drive back to hell the wolf, *Cupidigia*—*i.e.*, to repress the greedy ambition which had thrown the world into disorder, and to restore the Church to its original purity, the purity it had before the fatal gift of Constantine had begun to draw it into the arena of worldly politics.

Dante, therefore, seeks for the reversal of the whole course of policy by which the Church, especially after the time of Gregory the Great, had sought to establish its secular authority. He would strip the Church of her wealth in order to make her trust only in spiritual weapons. In the *Inferno*, Dante breaks out into taunts and rejoicings over the just fate of the simoniacal popes. "Tell me how much gold our Lord required of St. Peter, when He put the keys into his charge? Verily he demanded of him nought, but ' Follow me.' " [1] On the other hand, his intensest sympathy is reserved for the new orders of mendicant friars, who sought to bring back the simplicity of the Gospel, and his severest denunciations are for those who have corrupted the original purity of these orders, and of the Church in general.

This enables us to understand an often-discussed passage in which Dante puts among those contemptible beings—who " were neither faithful nor rebellious, but were for themselves," and who are therefore " hateful to God and to his enemies "— one who is characterised only as " the man who, through meanness, made the grand renunciation." [2] This we are told by all the older commentators of Dante refers to Pope Celestine, who resigned the papacy, and was succeeded by Boniface VIII. The contempt of Dante for this simple monk, who shrank from a burden which he could not bear, is to be understood only if we regard it as an expression of the disappointment of those who, in Celestine, saw a representative of the pure unworldly view of the functions of the Church lifted to the throne of Christendom, and who then saw him confess himself unequal to the mission thus committed to him. Dante sympathised with the

[1] *Inferno*, xix. 91.   [2] *Inferno*, iii. 60.

resentment of the so-called "spiritual Franciscans," those who sought to maintain, in all its strictness, the original law of St. Francis as to poverty— when, after a short interval, they saw worldly policy restored to the papal throne in the person of Boniface. Jacopone di Todi, the poet of the *Spiritual Brethren*, attacked Boniface with accusations of sacrilege, heresy and avarice, and in the *Paradiso* St. Peter is made to pronounce him a usurper. But for Celestine, whose selfish saintliness was not capable of sustaining contact with the world, and whose pusillanimity lost, as it seemed, the greatest of all opportunities, Dante reserves his bitterest word of contempt.

Now it is easy enough to see that Dante's ideal of a universal Church, standing side by side with a universal Empire, protected by the empire, and by its unworldliness saved from all collision therewith, was impracticable, was indeed incapable of realisation in *both* its aspects. The universality of the Empire was, even at the best, *magni nominis umbra*, and the assertion of its claims invariably brought it into collision with the privileges of the Church : and the Church, on the other hand, not seldom found itself driven to maintain those privileges by excommunicating the emperor and calling on his subjects to rebel. The emperors could not uphold law and order in their dominions without interfering with the spiritual courts and curtailing the rights of the clergy, and the popes saw no way of securing the independence of the Church except by asserting its claim to rule over the world. Thus the essential contradiction of the attempt to divide human life into two halves, and to determine definitely what was Cæsar's, and what was God's, showed itself in the logic of facts.

Yet undoubtedly the idea of such a separation, which would leave each in possession of all its legitimate prerogatives, and should completely secure it from coming into collision with the other, was the political ideal of the Middle Age, an ideal which was the necessary outcome of the way in which the Christian Church had for centuries been existing or endeavouring to exist, as a community in the world yet not of it. Hence Dante was only following out that ideal in its most logical form, when he demanded that the Church should return to its original purity, and should withdraw from all interference with the interests of the world, and that the Empire should again become all-powerful over man's secular life, as it seemed to have been before the Church became its rival. We might perhaps say that in this view of Dante's we find a culminating instance of the mediæval method of escaping all difficulties by a " Distinguo "— *i.e.*, of using a distinction to make a kind of truce between elements which it could not bring together in a true reconciliation. By absolutely separating the Empire and the Church, Dante conceived it to be possible to restore harmony between them.

And, indeed, it is true that such abstract opposites, if they could exist, would cease to come into collision, because they would cease to come into contact. Unfortunately, at the same time in which they thus cease to affect each other, they lose all meaning, as abstractions which have no longer any reference to the whole from which they were abstracted. Thus in Dante's treatise, *De Monarchia*, from which the above quotation is taken, the Empire is represented as an omnipotent justice, which, because omnipotent, has no special interest of its own, and therefore is freed from all temptation to injustice ; while the Church is conceived as reaching the same ideal purity by the opposite way—*i.e.*, by detaching itself from all finite interests whatever.

The real lesson to be learnt from such an abstract opposition is just the reverse of that to which it apparently points. It is that the opposing forces can never cease to be rivals, and are therefore never safe from impure compromises, until they are brought to a unity as complementary manifestations of one principle of life, which at once reveals itself

in their difference, and overcomes it. The problem is not to divide the world between God and
Cæsar, or, as we should now say, between God and
Humanity, but to give all to God in giving all to
Humanity, Humanity being conceived, not as a
collection of individuals, but as an organism in
which the Divine Spirit reveals Himself. Of this
solution there is no trace in Dante, nor could any
unbiassed interpreter suppose that, beneath the
form of adhesion to the mediæval duality of Church
and Empire, he conceals the idea of their essential
unity. What gives a colour of reason to such an
idea is merely that the new wine of Dante's poetry
does burst the old bottles of mediæval philosophy ;
or, in other words, that he so states the mediæval
ideal that he makes us see it to be in hopeless
antagonism with reality and with itself, and at the
same time to carry in it the germ of a new form of
social life.

3. A more definite anticipation of this new order
of ideas may, however, be found in Dante's treatment of the last of the three contrasts to which
reference has been made. It is true that Dante
repeats after St. Augustine and St. Thomas the
conception of a twofold truth, a truth of reason
which is determined by reason alone, and a truth
of faith which is primarily due to revelation. And
as a necessary consequence of this, he accepts the

idea of a twofold morality, a morality of the four
cardinal virtues, which are acquired by habit and
teaching on the basis of nature, and a morality of
the three *theological* virtues, which are entirely
the effect of supernatural inspiration.   Hence the
continually increasing danger and darkness of his
descent through the circles of the Inferno, and the
hopeful but slow and laborious nature of his ascent
over the terraces of the Purgatorial Hill, are put in
contrast with his swift upward flight through the
planetary heavens, in which he is conscious of no
effort, but only of the vision of Beatrice and of her
growing brightness.

But the theological barrier between the human
and the divine which Dante thus acknowledges,
and which, we may even say, he builds into the
structure of his poem, is removed or reduced to
a merely relative difference when we consider its
inner meaning.   In the exaltation of Beatrice, two
very different ideals of life are united, and two
different streams of poetry, which had run separate
up to the time of Dante, are concentrated in a
common channel.   The chivalrous worship of
woman, which grew up in connection with the
institutions of feudalism, is combined with that
adoration of divine love, as embodied in the Virgin
Mother, which gave tenderness to the piety of the
saints.   The hymn of worship, in which the pas-

sionate devotion of St. Francis and Jacopone di
Todi found utterance, absorbs into itself the love-
ballad of the Troubadour, and the imaginative
expression of natural feeling is purified and elevated by union with the religious aspirations of the
cloister.

Thus poetry brings ideas which had been separated by the widest " space in nature " to " join like
likes, and kiss like native things."   Dante's poetic
idealism—with that levelling power which is characteristic of all idealism, and above all of the
idealism of Christianity—sets aside all the hindrances that had prevented human and divine love
from coalescing.   Or, perhaps, we should rather
say that he approximates *as nearly* to this result as
the mediæval dualism will let him, retaining the
mark of his time only in the fact that the natural
passion which he idealises is one which was fed
with hardly any earthly food, but only with a few
words and looks, and which was soon consecrated
by death.   Thus the ascetic ideal of purity, which
shuns like poison the immediate touch of sense,
claims its tribute ; but when this tribute has been
paid, Dante has no further scruple in following
the impulse of natural emotion which bids him
identify his earthly love with the highest object of
his reverence, with the divine wisdom itself.
Thus, in the adoration of Beatrice, the Platonic

idealisation of ἔρως is interwoven with the Christian worship of a divine Humanity ; and a step is made towards that renewed recognition of the sacredness of natural feelings and relations, by which modern is distinguished from mediæval ethics.

Again, Dante accepts the mediæval idea of the superiority of the contemplative to the active life. This idea was the natural result of the ascetic and mystic view of religion which separates the love of God from the love of man, and regards the service of the latter as partly withdrawing our eyes from the direct vision of the former. " To love God *secundum se*," says St. Thomas, " is more meritorious than to love one's neighbour. Now, the contemplative life directly and immediately pertains to the love of God, while the active life directly points to the love of our neighbour." [1] Such a doctrine, if logically carried out, would involve an opposition of the universal principle of morality to all the particulars that ought to come under it ; or, to express the same thing theologically, it would involve a conception of God as a mere Absolute Being, who is not revealed in His creatures—a conception irreconcilable with the Christian idea of the unity of the divine and the human. The natural inference from such a conception would be that we must turn away from the finite in order to

[1] *Summa Theol.* ii. 2, 182.

bring ourselves into relation with the infinite.
But, in Dante, the identification of Beatrice with
the divine wisdom, or, what is the same thing, the
representation of the divine wisdom as individual-
ised and embodied—and that not merely in Christ
or in the saints, but in the human form that was
nearest to the poet's affection—practically counter-
acts this tendency, and involves a reassertion of the
positive side of Christianity as against the over-
emphasis which the Middle Age laid on its negative
side.

It may, indeed, be said that, for Dante, the
contemplative life remains still the highest.   But
this is not altogether true, at least in the sense in
which the above objection holds good.   For there
is a sense in which contemplation may be said to
include and go beyond action—that, viz., in which
religion includes and goes beyond morality.   Religion does not lift man *out of* the practical struggle
for good, but, in a sense, it lifts him *above* it.   It
turns morality from the effort after a distant and unattainable ideal into a consciousness of a divine
power within and without us, of which all things
are the manifestation ;   and so it enables us to
regard all things as working together for good,
even those that seem most to oppose it.   Religion
is thus primarily contemplative, not as looking
away from the world to God, nor as excluding the

active life of relation to the world, but because it is a rest in the consciousness that the ultimate reality of things, the world as seen *sub specie æternitatis*, is at once rational and moral. And such a consciousness, though it gives the highest inspiration to moral activity, does so by removing much of the pain of effort, and especially much of the feeling of hopelessness, which is apt to arise whenever moral effort is long continued against powerful obstacles.

So far, then, the addition of religion to morality tends to assimilate moral activity to Dante's swift and effortless ascent into heaven, to which, as we have seen, he is drawn upward simply by the vision of Beatrice. Not " I work," but " God worketh in me," is the genuine expression of religious feeling, and the source of its inspiring power. Dante puts the same idea in another way when he tells us that, if freed from the burden of sinful inclination, man cannot but follow the divine attraction of his nature, and inevitably rises to Paradise as to his natural place. " Thou shouldest not wonder at thy ascent," says Beatrice, " any more than that a stream descends from the top of the hill to the bottom. It would rather be a marvel if, freed from all impediment, thou didst remain below, *like living fire lying quietly on the ground*." [1]

[1] *Paradiso*, i. 139.

Thus in Dante's hands the one-sided exaltation of the contemplative life, which he accepts as part of the theological tradition of his time, becomes susceptible of an interpretation which removes all its one-sidedness. It is open for us to take it as expressing the truth that religion bases the " ought to be " of morality upon a deeper " is," and that the moral ideal is not merely a subjective hope or aspiration of the individual, but our best key to the nature of things. In a similar way the absolute distinction—which Dante, like the scholastic theologians whom he followed, is obliged to make—between the truths of faith and the truths of reason, finally resolves itself into this : that there are some truths which cannot be attained except by those " whose intelligence is ripened in the flame of love " [1]; or, in other words, some truths that must be felt and experienced before they can be known.

Considering all these points, we may fairly say that, orthodox as Dante is, his poem is the euthanasia of the dualistic theology and ethics of the Middle Ages. In spite of the horrors of his *Inferno*, which are the poetic reflection of the superstitious terrors of a half-barbarous age, and in spite of the monastic austerity and purity of his Paradise of light and music, which is like a glorified edition of the services of the Church,

[1] *Paradiso*, vii. 58.

Dante interprets the religion of the cloister in such a way as to carry us beyond it.   His *Divina Commedia* may be compared to the portal of a great cathedral, through which we emerge from the dim religious light of the Middle Ages into the open day of the modern world, but emerge with the imperishable memory of those harmonies of form and colour on which we have been gazing and with the organ notes that lifted our soul to heaven still sounding in our ears.

GOETHE AND PHILOSOPHY

THE Old Quarrel of Poetry and Philosophy—Relation of Poetic and Scientific Truth—Spontaneity of Poetry—Difference of its Idealism from that of Philosophy—Goethe's Debt to Philosophy and his Antagonism to it—His Self-limitation and indifference to Interests beyond the Limit—His Attitude towards Jacobi, Spinoza, Kant, Fichte and Schelling—His Early Revolt against the Mechanical Philosophy—His Sympathy with Rousseau—The First Poetic Period ending with *Werther*—Goethe's Turning from Rousseau to Spinoza—His Practical Optimism, and Objection to the Separation of the Natural and the Spiritual—His Love of Greek Art—His Relations with Schiller—Objective Thinking and Objective Poetry—His Opposition to Christianity—Gradual Modification of it in his Later Works.

THE "old quarrel of poets and philosophers," of which Plato speaks, is as far off from reconciliation as ever, and in one point of view we cannot wish it to be reconciled. It is far from desirable that poetry should ever become "a criticism of life," except in the sense in which beauty is always a criticism upon ugliness, or a good man upon a bad one ; and it is quite as undesirable that philosophy should relax any of its effort to produce such a criticism, or, in other words, to set the deeper meaning of things against their superficial appearances. Each does best service by remaining within its own limits and keeping to its own ways of action. Yet there is undoubtedly a point—and that, indeed, the highest point in both—in which they come into close relations with each other. Hence, at least in the case of the greatest poets, we are driven by a kind of necessity to ask what was their philosophy. A few words on the general relations of poetry and philosophy may make it easier to express what in this point of view we have to say about Goethe.

The poet, like the philosopher, is a seeker for truth, and we may even say for the same kind of truth. He may not, indeed, like the philosopher, separate the idea or principle from the immediate reality of things, but he must be so eager and passionate in his realism as to reach the ideal in it and through it. He must grasp the world of sense so firmly that it ceases to sting. If he remoulds the immediate facts of the world of experience, it must be by means of forces which are working in it as well as in himself, and which his own plastic genius only brings to clearer manifestation.

In some few cases, this poetic process of "widening nature without going beyond it," [1] has been so successful that it becomes almost a futile curiosity to ask what were the materials which the poet has used, or the bare facts for which he has substituted his creations. The kernel has been so completely extracted that we are not concerned about the husk. If we could learn the circumstances of the Trojan War as a contemporary historian might chronicle them, we should not know nearly so much of the inner movement and development of the Greek spirit as Homer has told us ; though we should probably find that Homer's story is nowhere a mere copy of the facts, but that it stands to them in somewhat the same relations in which the "Sorrows

[1] Schiller.

of Werther " stands to the accidents of Goethe's life in Welzlar, and the suicide of Jerusalem. The facts are changed, and a new world constructed out of the old by the shaping imagination of the poet, but the change is such that it seems to have taken place in the factory of Nature herself. The forces that work underground, and hide themselves from us beneath the appearances of human life, have, by the silent elaboration of poetic genius, forced their way to the surface, and transformed the appearances themselves. Hence the new creation has all the colours of life, and almost shames the so-called facts of every day by the sturdy force and reality of its presence. Thus before Shakespeare's characters most ordinary human beings seem like the shadows of the dead in Homer. It is not that in these dramas a different life is set before us from that which men everywhere lead, but the passions and characters which, in conflict with each other and with circumstance, gradually work out their destiny, are in the poet's mind put into a kind of forcing-house, and made with rapid evolution to show their inner law and tendency in immediate results.

It is indeed only the greatest poets who are capable of thus making themselves, at it were, into organs by which nature reaches a further development. In all but the greatest we find a mixture of

such creative reconstruction with what we can only
call manufacture.   The failing force of vision
obliges them to hold together by mechanical means
the elements which do not round themselves into
an organic whole.   And even to the greatest poets
it is not granted to have a complete and continuous
vision.   Hence, except in the case of short
" swallow-flights of song," which can be produced
in one lyric burst of feeling, works of *pure* poetic
art must be the result of much patient waiting and
watching for the spirit ; they cannot be perfected
without much self-restraint and critical rejection of
every element which is not quite genuine.   " That
which limits us, the common or vulgar," and which
by its presence at once turns poetry into prose,
cannot be excluded except by a self-abnegation as
great as that by which the scientific man puts aside
all subjective pre-suppositions and " anticipations
of nature."

For poetic truth does not lie on the surface any
more than scientific truth.   The *kinds* of truth are
indeed widely different.   The aim of the man of
science is to distinguish the threads of necessity
that bind together the most disparate phenomena,
and in pursuit of these he seems, to one who looks
at the immediate result, to be explaining away
all the life and unity of the world, and putting
everywhere mechanism for organism, even in the

organic itself. On the other hand, the poet ignores or endeavours to get beyond the external mechanism of the world ; he is ever seeking and finding life even among the dead. But only one who regards the abstractions of science as the ultimate truth of things, can take this process to be a mere play of subjective fancy, or can suppose that any great poetic creation is produced by an imagination which merely follows its own dreams and does not bend to any objective law. It is even harder for the poet to eliminate from his work all that is not living, than for the scientific man to set aside the phantoms of life, the final causes, which disturb the prose of science. In both cases the individual has to put himself aside and let nature speak ; but the poet listens for another voice, a " still small voice," which comes from a further depth. The extreme rarity of poetic works of a high order, in spite of the comparatively frequent appearance of a measure of poetic genius, shows how many and difficult are the conditions which must be satisfied in their production.

The poet, like the philosopher, is in search of a deeper truth in things than that which is the object of science. He seeks, as has been said, the unity and life which is hidden in the mechanism of the universe, and he who seeks truth in any form must be prepared for self-abnegating effort.

Yet we must not forget another characteristic of poetry by which it is separated at once from science and philosophy—viz., its spontaneous and even unconscious character. After all, the effort of the poet is to provide a free channel for a power that works in him like a natural force. Wordsworth's criticism of Goethe's poetry, that it was not "inevitable enough" (a criticism which is singularly wide of the mark in regard to the best of Goethe's work), is an apt expression of this truth. Creative imagination is a power which is neither lawless, nor yet, strictly speaking, under law ; it is a power which, as Kant said, *makes* laws. It carries us with free steps into a region in which we leave behind and forget the laws of nature ; yet, as soon as we begin to look round us and to reflect on our new environment, we see that it could not have been otherwise. The world has not been turned upside down, but widened by the addition of a new province which is in perfect continuity with it.

But this feat of "widening nature without going beyond it," has its special subjective conditions. It cannot be achieved by one in whom the division of man's higher and lower nature has produced the sense of an irreconcilable breach between the two, or in whose eyes their unity has been reduced to a mere ideal. Poetic genius must live in fruition, not in aspiration—must be at peace and not at war

with the world ; it must be able to see good in the
heart of evil, it must grasp as attained what others
see only as a distant hope.   The poet cannot be
one who has had to trample upon his natural life
in order to make room for moral freedom, or one
who has lost the vividness of the sensuous present
in order to grasp at an idea.   He must remain at
one with himself as in happy childhood, and maintain an unbroken life in spite of all fightings within
and contradictions without.   For if he does not, a
false note will get into his song ; it will become
a wail for a lost past, a complaint against time and
fortune, or an aspiration after the unattainable,
instead of an echo of the divine word that " all is
good."

Art must, therefore, in a sense, be joyous ; [1] if
it is not to fall beneath its idea, it must at least
return in its final note to joy.   If it admits the
tragic contrasts of life, it must not lose itself in
them ; it must carry us beyond " fear and terror,"
even if it has to carry us through them.   It must
not leave us victims of such passions without a
reconciling atonement, which makes us accept the
event, not merely as an inevitable fate, but as an
issue in which the dramatic evolution of character
has brought about *its own* destiny.   Thus, even
when it goes beyond the first and simplest theme of

[1] " Ernst ist das Leben, heiter ist die Kunst."   (Schiller.)

poetic imagination, and ceases to be an expression
of man's joy in the response of nature to the
demands of his spirit, it must restore the broken
harmony by giving us, even in the utmost tragic
catastrophe, the sense of the realisation of a law, in
which we are more deeply interested than even in
the sorrows and joys of the individual.   If, on the
contrary, a poem throws us back upon ourselves,
jarred and untuned as by a consciousness of inex-
plicable accident or meaningless sorrow, or if it
leaves us strained with a vacant longing for we
know not what, we may safely say that we have
been cheated by a false semblance of art, or at best
by an art which wilfully seeks to destroy the sources
of its own power.   For contradiction, division,
external limitation are the prose of life ; and art is
art, poetry is poetry, only as it disentangles, unites,
and reconciles, giving us, if not the open vision, at
least the presentiment or " Ahnung " of the unity
which is beneath and beyond it.

In a sense, then, we may admit that poetic art is
merely ideal.   It must be ideal just because it holds
so closely to the *immediate* reality or sensuous
presence of its objects, even while it lifts them
beyond those limits and conditions which are
attached to the things of sense.   It cannot therefore, even in tragedy, go fairly down into the
region of conflict and limitation, which, as I have

said, is the domain of prose. It shrinks from the abstractions and divisions of science, as fatal to that immediate unity and life which it cannot surrender. Hence its " old quarrel " with philosophy. Philosophy is, *in the end*, at one with poetry. It might even be said that *ultimately* it is nothing more than an attempt to prove that which poetry assumes as given, or to enable us by reflection to recognise as the universal principle of reality that ideal which poetry exhibits to us in special creations. Yet the essential differences of method make it difficult for two such disparate activities to come to any understanding with each other. Plato, in whom the perfect union of these two forms of spiritual life was most nearly realised, is also the writer who most strongly insists on their essential opposition. In truth they may be said to start in opposite directions, and only to coincide in their final goal.

For philosophy, whatever ultimately it may do to point towards unity, is obliged to begin by carrying abstraction and division to a further extent than even science. If it aims at a final synthesis, it is on the basis of an unsparing analysis : if it seeks to find a living unity in the world, it is not by restoring the immediate life, which science destroys that it may dissect the dead body. Rather its business is to complete the scientific disintegration that, through death, it may reach a higher life. It is essential to philosophy to separate the spiritual from the natural, the higher life from the lower life, the subject from the object, the universal from the particular, the ideal from the real. Thus it carries us deep into the region of abstraction and division, of contradiction and controversy ; and if it also can be said to carry us beyond that region, yet in this respect its work is never complete, and the answer it gives in one age requires to be, if not essentially changed, yet deepened and widened and translated into a new language with the changing experiences of another age. Thus the element of pure theory must always be a dangerous, and may even be a fatal, element to the poet ; for it severs that which it is his peculiar function to keep united, and even where it reunites, it has to accomplish its synthesis in a region of thought in which the sensuous forms of poetry can hardly breathe and live.

These general considerations may serve as an introduction to a few remarks on Goethe's attitude towards philosophy and its influence on his intellectual development.

Goethe owed much to particular philosophers ; we can often trace in his work indications of the study of Plato, and still more of Spinoza. Nor could he at any time withdraw himself from the influence of the great contemporaneous movement of idealistic thought, to which his own mental development moved in parallel lines, and on which it frequently reacted. But towards philosophy in general he preserved throughout his life a self-defensive attitude — a sort of armed neutrality. While he welcomed suggestions from it which were kindred with his own way of thinking, and even willingly appropriated many of its results, he always tried to keep his mind from being influenced by its methods and processes. He shrank from it, at first by a kind of instinct, and afterwards with the distinct conviction, that any nearer approach would be dangerous to that intuitive insight of imagination in which his own strength lay.

Such reserve and self-limitation were very characteristic of Goethe; for, notwithstanding his many-sidedness, no one ever realised more distinctly the necessity of keeping within his own province. That each one must know himself in the sense of knowing his work, and must refuse to allow himself to be drawn away to interests and pursuits which lie beyond the range of his faculty, was for him the first maxim of self-culture. His obedience to it has often subjected him to serious moral charges, on the ground that his pursuit of self-culture involved a narrow self-absorption and a selfish indifference to the interests of his nation or of humanity. Such a view might appeal to expres-

sions like the following in a letter to Lavater:
" The passion to lift the pyramid of my being, the
basis of which is assigned and established for me, as
high as possible into the air, outweighs everything
else, and permits me scarcely for one moment to
forget it." But we must interpret an exaggerated
phrase like this by Goethe's often-expressed conviction that we necessarily become bunglers and
meddlers, when we interfere with that which lies
beyond the " orbit fixed for our existence by
eternal laws." Activity that does not advance our
own self-culture will, he holds, be useful to no
other man. For him, as for Plato, all the virtues
were summed up in each one doing his own business, and avoiding interference with the business of
others.

On this principle we can, at least, partly explain
what gave so much offence to the patriotism of
his countrymen—his attitude during the war of
liberation. In the *Awakening of Epimenides*, a
poem which was written after the victory over
Napoleon, and in which he expresses a kind of
penitence for his silence during the national
struggle, he suggests the excuse that the part he
was called by his nature to play was, not to share
in the war, but to prepare for the higher civilisation
that should arise after the war was ended. Epimenides, who represents Goethe, is made to say:

" I am ashamed of the hours of rest ; it would have been a gain to suffer with you ; for the pain you have borne makes you greater than I." But the answer of the priest is : " Blame not the will of the Gods that thou hast gained many a year ; they have kept thee in quietness so that thy feeling may be pure (*dass du rein empfinden kannst*). And thus thou art in harmony with the future days to which history offers our pain and sorrow, our endeavour and our courage."

It was a similar feeling that made Goethe generally keep philosophy, as it were, at arm's length, while at the same time he recognised the points of contact which it offered to him. In a letter to Jacobi he says : —

"You can easily imagine my attitude to philosophy. When it lays itself out for division, I cannot get on with it ; indeed I may say that it has occasionally done me harm by disturbing me in my natural course. But when it unites, or rather, when it confirms our original feeling as though we were one with Nature, and elevates it into a peaceful intuition that under its external $\sigma\acute{\nu}\gamma\kappa\rho\iota\sigma\iota\varsigma$ and $\delta\iota\acute{\alpha}\kappa\rho\iota\sigma\iota\varsigma$ a divine life is present to us, even if we are not permitted to lead such a life ourselves—then it is welcome to me, and you may reckon upon my sympathy."

From this we may explain the charm which he found in the one philosophical work from the influence of which he never tried to withdraw himself — the *Ethics* of Spinoza. That strange book, in which the soul of poetry is clothed in the body of geometry, took hold of Goethe at an early period, so soon as he had begun to emerge out of the " storm and stress " of his youth; and through all his subsequent life he continued to refresh and strengthen himself with its doctrine of all embracing unity and disinterested love. The extreme antagonism of Spinoza's methods of thinking and expression to his own contributed to the attraction. He saw in Spinoza his intellectual complement, whom he could enjoy without being in any way tempted to go beyond himself.

"His all-reconciling peace contrasted with my all-agitating endeavour ; his intellectual method was the opposite counterpart of my poetic way of feeling and expressing myself; and even the inflexible regularity of his logical procedure, which might be considered ill-adapted to moral subjects, made me his most passionate scholar and his devoted adherent. Mind and heart, understanding and sense, were drawn together with an inevitable elective affinity, and this at the same time produced an intimate union between individuals of the most different type."

Goethe never attempted to master the Spinozistic philosophy as a system ; he tells us, indeed, that he never even read the *Ethics* through at one time. But he kept reading *in* it, as people read in the Bible, to get strength and inspiration, and to confirm himself in those principles which gradually had become almost identified with his consciousness of himself. No other philosophy ever came so close to him : though his early association with Herder brought him indirectly under many philosophic influences, and in particular we often find him using the ideas and language of Leibniz.

To the Critical philosophy, in which the subject seemed to be set against the object and the ideal separated from the real, he at first felt an instinctive repulsion. But, at a later time, intercourse with Schiller, who professed himself a Kantian but who tried to soften Kant's sharp contrast between the moral and the natural, did something to remove his objections. And the *Critique of Judgment*, in which Kant himself undertakes the same task of mediation between freedom and nature, was a book almost entirely to his mind. He detected the way in which Kant, especially in this final development of his philosophy, points ('' as by a side gesture '') beyond the limitations which he seems to fix for the intelligence of man, and with a curious turning of the tables, he claimed Kant's account of the '' intuitive understanding '' as a fit description of the true synthetic method for the discovery of nature's laws which he had himself followed.

On the other hand, he was repelled by the one-

sided Idealism of Fichte, who exaggerated that
aspect of the critical philosophy with which he was
least in sympathy, and he seldom speaks of " the
great Ego of Ossmanstadt " without a shade of
irony.   There is even a trace of malicious satisfaction in the way in which he relates how Fichte had
his windows broken by the students of Jena : "not
the most pleasant way of becoming convinced of
the existence of a *non-ego*."   The further development of the ideas of the *Critique of Judgment*, by
which Schelling brought Idealism, so to speak, into
line with Spinozism, excited his eager interest, and
he even speaks of the advance of philosophy as
having helped him to reconcile himself to many
things that had repelled him at an earlier time, and
especially as having considerably changed his view
of Christianity.   Still, on the whole, except in the
case of Spinoza, his attitude to philosophy is that
of an outsider who accepts its help when it seems
to support his own way of thinking, but disregards
it when it does not.   And his ultimate view of
it seems to be that indicated by the (somewhat
ambiguous) aphorism, that " man is not born to
solve the problem of the universe, but to find out
wherein it consists."

What has just been said may be taken as a summary of Goethe's relations to philosophy.   Such a
summary, however, can tell us very little about

Goethe, unless we are able to bring it into definite relation with the different stages of his intellectual history. In this article we can only attempt to indicate one or two turning-points in that history, and especially to show how it was that, at one of these turning-points, the philosophy of Spinoza gained so great a power over him, and how subsequently it combined itself with other influences to produce that distinctive cast of thought which we trace in his later works.

The first question we are naturally led to ask about an original genius like Goethe, who has done so much to change the main current of European thought, is as to his relation to the past. Against what had he to revolt—from what had he to free himself, in order to open the way for the new life that was in him? And on the other side, with what already acting forces could he ally himself?

Born in the middle of the eighteenth century, he awakened to intellectual life between a lifeless orthodoxy and an external enlightenment, which was gradually undermining it, but at the same time reducing itself to a platitude. Looking beyond his own country to France, which had then all the prestige of culture, he found an artificial and aristocratic literature which repelled his youthful sympathies, and a scepticism which, stopping short in its development and allying itself with the rising

mathematical and physical sciences, was on the way
to produce a mechanical theory of the universe.
He had soon got by heart the negative lesson of
Voltaire, and, like Faust, he found that, while it
freed him from all his superstitions, it at the same
time made the world empty and barren to him.
And the mechanical philosophy which presented
itself in the *Système de la Nature*, as the positive
substitute for his lost faith, could not but fill a
poet's soul with pious horror.   In Goethe's autobiography, though written many years after, we can
still discern the vehemence of his revolt against a
theory which '' reduced that which appears higher
than nature, or rather as the higher nature in
nature itself, to aimless and formless matter and
motion.''

"It appeared to us," he declared, "so grey, so Cimmerian,
and so dead that we shuddered at it as at a ghost.   We
thought it the very quintessence of old age.   All was said
to be necessary, and therefore, no God.   Why, we asked,
should not a necessity for God find its place among other
necessities ?   We confessed, indeed, that we could not
withdraw ourselves from the necessary influences of day
and night, of the seasons, of the climatic changes, of
physical and animal conditions ; yet we felt something
within us that appeared arbitrarily to assert itself against
all these; and again something which sought to counter-
poise such arbitrariness and to restore the equilibrium
of life."

On the other hand, the ordinary teleological theology, with its external world-architect and externally determined designs, could not seem to Goethe any more satisfactory than the mechanical philosophy. It had, indeed, the same fault as that philosophy ; for it too substituted an external composition of parts for life and development. He had put such theology away from him almost in his boyhood, and he could not return to it. Then as always, he was ready to shoot Voltairian shafts of wit at a doctrine of final causes, which turned any accidental result of the existence of an object into its end.

In this state of mind, the fiery appeals of Rousseau to *nature*, as a power within man which is self-justified against every constraint forced upon him from without, could not but produce the greatest effect on Goethe. All his discontent with an unproductive orthodoxy, and all his distaste for a disintegrating scepticism, combined to make him accept a creed which promised freedom to all the forces of his being. Rousseau seemed to vindicate the claims of everything that had life, and to war only with the dead ; and a susceptible poetic nature, doubting of itself, was only too willing to be re-assured by him as to the rightness of its own impulses. The vagueness of this gospel of nature was for a time hidden from Goethe by the very

intensity of the poetic impulse within him, which
responded vividly to every impression from without. " See, my friend," he writes in an early
letter, " what is the beginning and end of all my
writing, but the reproduction of the world around
me by an inward cosmic principle which seizes
upon everything, binds it together, new creates it,
kneads it, and sets it out again in its own form
and manner." The rush of youthful inspiration
seemed to need no guide ; and it spent its force,
in every direction from which excitement came,
with what Goethe afterwards called " a divine
wantonness." The calm pages of the *Dichtung
und Wahrheit* preserve only a feeble image of the
fervour and passion which is shown in the letters
and poems of this time of " storm and stress."
From some of the worst dangers of such a time,
Goethe was saved by the genuineness of his poetic
impulse. But such a living at random, with all
sails set and no hand on the helm, could not long
be possible even to genius. In his case it resulted
in a crisis of sensibility, the image of which is
preserved for us in the *Sorrows of Werther*, a work
in which he gave a final expression to the passions
and illusions of his youth, and so, once for all, freed
himself from them.

" Nature " is the obvious rallying cry of a new
generation striving to free itself from the weight

of the ideas and institutions of an earlier time. Such a cry may often be the expression of a very artificial and sophistical state of mind, which, beginning in the desire to throw off that which is really oppressive, ends in a fretful revolt against the most necessary conditions of human life. The vague impulse of youth which refuses to limit itself or give up its " natural right to all things," the vain demand of the heart to find an outward world which corresponds to its wants, the rebellion of passion against the destiny which refuses it an immediate satisfaction, the hatred of the untamed spirit for everything of the nature of convention and rule—each and all of these feelings readily disguise themselves under the name of a desire to *return to nature.*

But in truth such a longing can least of all be satisfied with the simple rustic and domestic life which it seems to admire. When it cries out— " *O fortunatos nimium, sua si bona norint!* "—it forgets that knowledge would be fatal to such bliss. The self-absorbed, self-conscious spirit, preying upon itself in its isolating individualism, is least of all capable of that simple union with others for which it pines, of that contentment with natural pleasures which it loves to express. Rude nature would terrify it most of all, if it could once fairly come in contact with her. The discontent of the

sentimentalist with the world is merely a way of
expressing what is really the inner self-contradiction of his own state.   The exaggerated image of
self stands between him and the world, and gives
rise to an infinite craving which spurns every finite
satisfaction.   His joy is, in the language of
Goethe, a fruit which is " corrupted ere it is broken
from the tree."

This strange emotional disease, which has so
long vexed the modern world, has had its literary
representatives in most European nations, and has
been expressed by them with many national and
individual modifications.   From Rousseau, whose
whole individuality was absorbed by it, it received
its first and most complete literary embodiment.
In this country, Byron combined it with the fervour
of an active temperament, and draped it in a somewhat theatrical costume.   Goethe, in his *Werther*,
gave to it a purer rendering, combining it with the
domestic sentiment and reflective self-analysis of
his nation.

But, while Rousseau and even Byron were
permanent victims of the self-contradictory state
of feeling which they expressed, Goethe, in his
Werther, found a true æsthetic deliverance from it.
He cured himself, so to speak, by painting his
disease.   He exorcised the spectre that barred his
way to a higher life by forcing it to stand to be

painted. *Werther* was his demonstration to himself of the emptiness and unworthiness of a state of mind, whose only legitimate end was suicide. This, indeed, was not understood at the time. Goethe was haunted through life by the " *vielbeweinter Schatten* "—by a constant demand for sympathy from those whose malady he had so perfectly described, and who expected to find in him a fellow-sufferer. But for him, the writing of the book was the beginning of recovery. In his autobiography, he complains of those who sought a direct moral lesson in a work of art, and who imagined that *Werther* was intended to justify the sentimentality and the suicide of the hero. For himself, however, it had a lesson, the reverse of that which lies on the surface of it— the lesson that rebellion against the conditions of human life is not only futile, but irrational. In these limiting conditions, he is never weary of preaching, lies the way to freedom. " From the law that binds all men, he only can be freed who overcomes himself." How far this lesson was revealed to Goethe in the mere rebound from Wertherism, and how far he owed it to any external teaching, we cannot now disentangle. It is sufficient to say that he seemed to himself to find it in the pages of Spinoza. Goethe's " apprenticeship," to use his own metaphor, was ended, when

Spinoza took in his inner life that place which had hitherto been filled by Rousseau. The passage in the *Dichtung und Wahrheit* in which this is expressed is familiar, but it is necessary to quote it here once more :—

"Our physical as well as our social life, morality, custom, knowledge of the world, philosophy, religion— yea, many an accidental occurrence—all tell us that we must *renounce*. So much is there that belongs to our inmost being, which we cannot develop and form outwardly ; so much that we need from without for the completion of our being is withdrawn from us: and, again, so much is forced on us which is both alien and burdensome. We are deprived of that which is toilsomely won, of that which is granted by kindly powers, and ere we can see the meaning of it, we find ourselves compelled to give up our personality, first by fragments, and then completely. In such cases it is usual to pay no attention to any one who makes faces at the sacrifice exacted of him ; rather, the bitterer the cup, the sweeter must be one's bearing, in order that the unconcerned spectator may not be annoyed by a grimace.

" To solve this hard problem, nature has furnished man with a rich provision of force, activity, and toughness. But what most often comes to his help is his unconquerable levity. By this he becomes capable of renouncing particular things at each moment, if he can only grasp at something new in the next. Thus unconsciously we are constantly renewing our whole lives. We put one passion in place of another ; business, inclinations, amusements, hobbies, we prove them all one after another, only to cry out that 'all is vanity.' No one is shocked at this false, nay, blasphemous, speech; nay, every one thinks that in uttering it he has said something wise and unanswerable. Few, indeed, are those who are strong enough to anticipate such unbearable feelings, and in order to escape from all partial renunciations, to perform one all-embracing act of renunciation. These are the men who convince themselves of the existence of the eternal, of the necessary, of the universal, and who seek to form conceptions which cannot fail them, yea, which are not disturbed, but rather confirmed, by the contemplation of that which passes away. But as there is something superhuman in this attitude of mind, such persons are commonly held to be inhuman, without God and aliens to the world, and it is much if men refrain from decorating them with horns and claws."

" Renunciation once for all in view of the Eternal." It was this lesson that made Goethe feel an " atmosphere of peace breathe upon him," whenever he opened his Spinoza. Much may be said in some respects against Goethe's moral attitude, but there is one point in which it is scarcely possible to praise it too much. No one ever acted more faithfully on the resolve to make the best of circumstances, and to put behind him with resolute cheerfulness the " blasphemous speech that all is vanity."

It is easy in one way to make too much of one's

own life, but it is not easy to make enough of it in Goethe's sense of living in the present, and drawing all the good out of it. Where men do not live from hand to mouth, nor are the victims of one narrow interest, their self-occupation is often a dreaming about the past and the future, which isolates them from other men and from the world. "They are always losing to-day, because there has been a yesterday, and because to-morrow is coming." "They little suspect what an inaccessible stronghold *that* man possesses, who is always in earnest with himself and with the things around him." To be "always in earnest" with little things as well as great, with the minutest facts presented to his observation as with the most important issues of life, to throw the whole force of his being into a court masque, (when that was the requirement of the hour), as into a great poem or a scientific discovery ; to be, in short, always intent upon the "nearest duty," was Goethe's practical philosophy.

With this was combined a resolute abstinence from complaint, or even from thought about what was not granted to him by nature and fortune, and an eager and thankful acceptance of what was so granted. In one way, this "old heathen," as he calls himself, is genuinely pious ; he is always acknowledging his advantages and opportunities, and almost never speaking of hindrances ; and he seems constantly to bear with him a simple-hearted confidence in the goodness and justice of the Power, which has brought him just what it has brought, and refused just what it has refused. He belongs to the order of which he speaks in the second part of *Wilhelm Meister*, the order of those who "cheerfully renounce" whatever is not granted to them, and who come back through a kind of Stoicism to an Optimism which moves on a higher level. With this was connected an ungrudging recognition of the excellences of others, and an unenvious readiness to further every one in his own way. It was this pliant strength, and the faith on which it rests, that alone could have attracted to Goethe the admiration and almost worship of a man like Carlyle, who, in all superficial interests, was at the opposite pole of thought and temperament.

Goethe's "storm and stress" period—the period of "unconditioned effort to break through all limitations," as he calls it — was ended with *Werther*, and with it began a movement towards limit and measure, which culminated at the period of his Italian journey. If in this new phase of thought nature was still worshipped, it was no longer regarded as a power that reveals itself at once in the immediate appearances of the outward

world, or the immediate impulses of the human
spirit.   It was now the *natura naturans* of Spinoza
—*i.e.*, as Goethe conceived it, a plastic organising
force which works secretly in the outward and
especially in the organic world, and which in
human life reveals itself most fully as the ideal
principle of art.   Clinging, as an artist, to the
external, Goethe now sees that the truth of nature
does not lie immediately on the surface, but in a
unity which can be grasped only by a penetrative
insight.   Demanding, as a poet, that the ideal
should not be separated from the sensuous, he is
now conscious that the poetic truth of the passions
shows itself, not in their immediate expression, but
only when their conflict leads to their " purification," and so reveals a higher principle.

Hence, though, even more decidedly than at an
earlier time, he rejects the Christian faith, which
he regards as breaking the sacred bond of nature
and Spirit, and setting the one against the other,
it is an idealised materialism which he opposes to
it.   What he fears and abhors in religion and in
philosophy is the idea of " a godless nature and
an unnatural God," [1] a mechanical world-order and
an external world-architect or world-governor who
" lets the world swing round his finger."   " It
befits Him to move the world from within, to

[1] Schelling.

cherish nature in Himself, and Himself in nature, so that what lives and moves and is in Him never forgets His force or His spirit." He is filled with the thought of a Power which manifests itself in the facts of nature, though only to an eye which can penetrate through the apparent chaos to the point where it may be seen as a cosmos. The great modern ideas of organism and development have taken hold upon him, and he regards the artistic faculty as simply the highest expression of the shaping principle which works underground in nature. His fundamental ideas might be summed up in the pregnant words of Shakespeare—

> "Nature is made better by no mean,
> But nature makes that mean : so o'er the art,
> Which you say adds to nature, is an art
> That nature makes."

He had come, he tells us, " to regard his own indwelling poetic power as simply and entirely nature," and as with him " every idea rapidly changed itself into an image," he sought to express his religious attitude by a new rendering of the old myth of Prometheus. He too, like Prometheus, had a consciousness of " the god within him " which made him independent of the gods above ; for his poetic faculty seemed to him something higher than his individual will and impulses—

something that might claim kindred with the productive force of nature itself.

Such a view of things we may call in a special sense Hellenic, since it was in ancient Greece that the higher spiritual interests of man seemed most directly to connect themselves with the gifts of nature. The Greeks were led by an almost unconscious impulse to idealise the natural without ever breaking with it or opposing the spiritual to it. Thus they showed themselves artists not only in art, but in life, and escaped the painful division of the modern mind.

"The modern," writes Goethe, " can scarcely bend his thoughts upon any object without throwing himself into the infinite, in order finally, if things go well with him, to return to a limited point ; but the ancients, without traversing any such circuitous path, felt all their individual requirements satisfied within the limits of the beautiful world. Wherefore are their poets and historians the wonder of those who understand, the despair of those who would imitate them, but because the *dramatis personæ* whom they had to set on the stage took so deep an interest in their own immediate selves, in the narrow sphere of their Fatherland, in the course of their own lives and that of their fellow citizens—because, in short, with all their heart and soul they threw themselves upon the present ? Hence it could not be difficult for writers who were filled with a kindred spirit to make such a present eternal. What actually happened had for them that magic value, which we are scarcely able to attach to anything but that which is thought and felt. They clung so closely to what is nearest, what is truest and most real, that even their fancy pictures have bone and marrow. Man and what is human were most highly prized, and all man's inward and outward relations to the world were exhibited as powerfully as they were apprehended. For not yet were thought and feeling dismembered by abstraction ; not yet had that scarcely remediable division been produced in the sound nature of man."[1]

These words bear the impress of the change by which Goethe passed from what is usually called the romantic to the classic school of art. From his earliest years indeed he had felt the charm of Greek art and poetry ; but the productions of his youth were animated by another spirit. *Götz von Berlichingen*, his first important dramatic work, was one of the earliest expressions of that passion for mediæval ideals which afterwards went so far in Germany and other countries ; and his first essay on art was an enthusiastic tribute to the glories of Strasburg Cathedral. Most of the poetic works attempted or sketched out in this period, such as *The Wandering Jew* and the first outline of *Faust*, show the same bent of mind ; and in *Werther* the endless lament of modern

[1] Goethe's *Essay on Winckelmann*.

sentimentalism over the separation of the real from
the ideal reached its *ne plus ultra* of expression.
But with this work Goethe, as we have seen, made
a return upon himself, and almost violently rejected
from him the ideas and methods of romanticism.
He became the sworn enemy of all formless and
chaotic productions, and insisted with growing
emphasis upon the necessity of form and measure.
It is a superficial indication of this that he began
to versify his dramatic works, even those that had
at first been composed in prose, and in many cases
to select classic subjects and use classic metres.

The same change showed itself in other contemporaneous writers, as, for example, in Schiller,
whose *Götter Griechenlands* is an expression of
that admiration for the repose and harmony of the
antique, which was awakened in him in the reaction
against the untamed violence of *The Robbers*.
But it is characteristic that while Schiller expresses
this feeling as a longing for something unattainable
—something that has once for all been taken from
men by the progress of human thought and can
never be perfectly recovered—Goethe has no such
word of despair.   For him the ideal is there before
us in nature for our eyes to see, if they can only
look deep enough, and now, as in Greece, it is
working in the poet's mind, and reproducing itself
in art.   His dawning friendship with Schiller was

disturbed when the latter began to insist upon the Kantian doctrine, that no experience can ever be adequate to an idea. Goethe reflected, however, that if Schiller held that to be an idea which he expressed as experience, there must be some mediating link between them. "I told him that I was glad to think that I had ideas without knowing it, and that I could even see them with my eyes."

This last expression has immediate reference to Goethe's scientific views, especially in relation to the Metamorphosis of Plants. This, like all his contributions to biology, was inspired by the idea that there is a unity of principle in all life, and that it develops toward diversity by continuous modification of a single form. This idea led him to regard all plants as variations on a single type, and all the parts of each plant as correlative modifications of one simple form by which it has been adapted to various functions. The same principle guided him to the discovery of the traces in man of the intermaxillary bone, the absence of which had been supposed to distinguish the structure of man from that of the apes, and also made him one of the first to maintain that all parts of the skull are modified vertebræ. Thus, in spite of his being in a technical sense an amateur in science, Goethe grasped the idea of development, and used it to throw light upon the animal kingdom, when as yet few or none of the professed biologists had reached such a point of view.

Nor did he regard these biological studies as a something distinct from his poetic work. On the contrary, he conceived them to be a necessary complement or continuation of that work, and he complained of the imperfect insight of some of his friends, who thought that he was wasting time upon scientific studies that might have been better spent in poetic creation, and who did not detect how this interest "sprang out of his inmost being." [1]   And when an eminent naturalist complimented him on his " objective thinking "—*i.e.*, on his power of giving himself up to the sensuous impressions of objects in such a way as to extract their secret—he did not hesitate to claim for himself in the same sense the power of being objective in poetry (*Gegenständliche Dichtung*) :—

" Certain great motives, legends, ancient traditions so deeply impressed themselves upon my mind, that I kept them living and active within me for thirty or forty years. To me it appeared the most beautiful of possessions to see such worthy images renewed in my imagination, in which they were, indeed, continually transformed, yet without being altered, till at last they were raised to a purer form and a more definite expression."

These words well express the manner of Goethe's

[1] *Campaign in France*, November, 1792.

poetic production. It was not his way, as it was
the way of Schiller, to concentrate his thoughts
upon a subject, and force his genius into action.
Rather he watched the creations as they grew
within him, and used his conscious intelligence
only to defend the work from all incongruous
elements.

Such "objective poetry" cannot be an easy
matter even for the greatest of poets. As it takes
much metaphysic to keep free from metaphysic,
so it requires no little critical and reflective power
in the poet to purge out the dross of prose from
his work, and especially to free its pure intuitive
unity from the artifice and mechanism of reflection.
Above all it requires a certain stubborn faith in the
"whispers of the lonely muse when the whole
world seems adverse," a resolute maintenance of
the consciousness of poetic harmony in the face of
all the discords of life, which is hard for the poet,
just in proportion as the very condition of his
existence is his susceptibility to impression. And
for the modern poet this is harder than for the
ancient, because the movement of history has
brought with it new problems and causes of division. The greater the conflict of man's nature
with itself and with circumstances, the more
difficult has become the artist's task of making
music out of the jarring forces in and around him,

and preventing their confusion and conflict from mingling with his song.

In a passage already quoted, as in many others, Goethe expresses his sense of the effort which the modern requires to make in order to place and keep himself at a point of view which the Greek took up almost by instinct. And it is indeed this effort itself, and the consciousness of it, which prevents Goethe from ever being wholly Greek. Even in those of his works that are most filled with the spirit of antiquity, he is obliged to pay this tribute to the time. He is not a Greek, because, in order to reach the " peace and purity of the antique," he has to conquer an antagonism which for the Greek did not exist. This feeling is expressed half-humorously in his account of a conversation with Schiller, who regarded the Fall as a desirable event, because only by it could man rise above his animal innocence ; while Goethe maintained that such a break in the continuity of development was a disaster. In the same spirit he sometimes spoke of the Reformation as a violent crisis which delayed the progress of civilisation, and condemned the Revolutionary struggle of his own day as a disturbance to peaceful culture. " I hate all violent overturns, because in them men lose as much as they gain. All that is violent and precipitate displeases me, because it is not conformable to nature. In politics, as in nature, the true method is to wait." Struggle, warfare, revolution is to him the negative and the barren ; and even patriotism, with its exaltation of one nation at the expense of another, is a doubtful virtue. "How could I take up arms without hate?" he cries. "National hate is a particular hate ; it is in a lower region that it is most energetic and ardent ; but there is a height at which it vanishes, when one is, so to speak, above nationalities, and one feels the happiness and misery of a neighbouring people as his own."

This idea of all negation, controversy, and conflict as something essentially evil is embodied in his wonderful creation of Mephistopheles, the disintegrating spirit who is continually warring against life and energy, but who is tolerated by the divine power, because man is so fond of "unconditioned peace," and requires to be fretted and provoked into activity. Even so much toleration as this, however, is for God and not for man, who is called to "hate the devil and him only," to withdraw himself from all that is negative, violent, and destructive, and to devote all his life to that which is positive and productive, and who thus only can hope for a final deliverance from the base companion who is allowed in this world to haunt him.

"Gerettet ist das edle Glied
    Der Geisterwelt vom Bösen :
    Wer immer strebend sich bemüht
    Der können wir erlösen."

It is here, perhaps, that we find the limitations
of the genius of Goethe, limitations which were
closely connected with the sources of his strength.
As to the artist the immediate sensuous form of
reality is indispensable, so Goethe was jealous of
any influence that tends to mar or destroy it.
Division, pain, and evil appeared to him too great
a price to pay even for the highest good, and, in
the spirit of his master Spinoza, he was inclined to
deny that such a price was necessary. He demanded that the highest should be attained without
a breach with nature, and merely by continuing
her work upon a higher platform. Hence he was
repelled from history, as he was repelled from
politics, by the violence of the struggles, the depth
of the divisions, and the greatness of the sacrifices
with which the progress of man is purchased.
Hence also he could not accept the Christian idea
of life.

It is true, as we have seen, that he was inspired
with the great moral idea of renunciation, but his
interpretation of it is somewhat different from the
Christian interpretation. He does not exactly bid
us die to self that we may live ; he bids us re-

nounce all that nature and fortune refuse us, in the confidence that if we keep working on to the end " nature will be obliged to give us another form of existence when that which we have can no longer contain our spirit." The difference may seem almost verbal, and it is easy to see that by a slight change of tone the one lesson may be made to pass into the other. Nay, we may even say that such a change of tone is perceptible in some of the later works of Goethe himself. But in the first instance, the variation of expression concealed a real difference of spirit. It showed that Goethe feared and shrank from what has been called " the earnestness, the pain, the patience and the labour of the negative," through which the Christian spirit reaches a higher affirmative ; that he could not reconcile himself to a war with nature even as the way to a higher reconciliation.

This difference between the Goethean and the Christian idea of life showed itself in the most marked way in Goethe after his Italian journey. At that time he was so imbued with the naturalistic spirit of antiquity that he regarded the productions of mediæval art as for the most part monstrosities, or at least as eccentricities that were not to be copied. He even felt and occasionally expressed a violent repulsion towards the symbols of Christian worship and took pleasure in proclaiming himself a " heathen."

At a later period the bitterness of this antagonism disappeared. As his exclusive Hellenism
was gradually modified by advancing years he
became ready to admit the value and even the
supreme moral importance of Christian ideas. " It
is altogether 'strange to me," he writes to Jacobi,
in reference to the dramatist Werner, " that I, an
old heathen, should see the Cross planted in my
own ground, and hear Christ's blood and wounds
poetically preached, without its offending me. We
owe this to the higher point of view to which
philosophy has raised us." His " truly Julian
hate to Christianity and so-called Christians," he
declared on one occasion, with a touch of humour,
had softened itself with years, so that little was
wanting to make him say with the Ethiopian
eunuch in the Acts, " What doth hinder me to be
baptised! " And in the *Wanderjahre*, he makes
a broad distinction between the " ethnic religions "
and the religion which teaches " reverence for that
which is beneath us," recognising in the latter the
highest of all religions. He adds, however, that
it must not be understood to exclude the other two
religions—the religion of reverence for that which
is above us, and the religion of reverence for
equals. The overseer of his ideal educational
institution, when asked which religion he accepts,
has to answer : " Alle drei "—each and all of the

three religions that have divided man's allegiance in the past.

In truth Goethe's quarrel with Christianity was due to two causes which were at first closely connected, but which are capable of being separated. In the first place, as has been suggested above, it was due to his viewing Christianity as a religion of the other world, a religion whose God was not the principle of all life in nature and man, but an external creator and governor. In the second place, it was due to the prominence of the ascetic or negative element in Christianity, and to the divorce of the natural and spiritual which is connected therewith.

Now the first of these objections rested on a mental characteristic which Goethe could scarcely have surrendered without ceasing to be Goethe, the born enemy of all that is transcendent, all that carries us into a region beyond the possibility of human experience. It was the vocation of Goethe's life to teach that what in this sense cannot be brought within our reach, is as good as nothing for us. His objection to Christianity on this ground, therefore, could be removed only in so far as he was led by the philosophical movement of his time to attach greater importance to the Christian idea of the unity of the divine and the human, and to regard the purely supernatural element as an accident.

On the other hand, Goethe's objection to Christianity as a negative and ascetic religion became greatly modified when, in later years, the Greek conception of life ceased to be all-sufficient for him. Ultimately, as we have seen, he came to admit the necessity of a religion of reverence for that which is beneath us—a religion which could see the divine even in that which in its immediate aspect is "repulsive, hateful, and evil." But that which is "repulsive, hateful, and evil" cannot by any gradual transition be elevated and refined to goodness. If the divine is to be revealed in it, it can only be by the negation of that which at first it seems to be. The Christian idea of self-realisation through self-sacrifice is the necessary outcome of the religion of reverence for that which is beneath us. Hence we do not wonder to find Goethe in the same connection treating the *Sanctuary of Sorrow*, in which the sufferings and death of Christ are represented, as the innermost sanctuary of religion. Into this sanctuary, however, he avoids taking us. He is, one might say, theoretically reconciled with Christianity, but something still repels him from it. He waits, to use the imagery of his *Märchen*, till the narrow fisherman's hut shall become the altar in a new temple of humanity. The form in which Christianity is commonly presented as a religion of supernaturalism and other-worldliness continues to keep him alienated from that which in its moral essence he recognises as the highest.

Perhaps we may best sum up what has to be said of Goethe by calling him the most modern of the moderns, the high priest of a culture which, in its opposition to mediævalism, is carried back towards the literature of the Greeks, " the most human and humane of literatures, the literature of those who were most at home in the world." It was characteristic of the mediæval mind to seek for that which is highest in that which is furthest removed from man, that which can least be brought within the range of human experience. The divine power on which it depended for the elevation of man, was conceived as acting upon him from without, as upon a lifeless and inert material. The asceticism, the supernaturalism, the divided life of the Middle Ages, were only the natural result of such conceptions.

On the other hand, the whole movement of civilisation from the time of the revival of learning has been a war against such ways of thinking. The modern spirit, like the spirit of antiquity, is obliged, by its most essential intellectual instincts, to cling to that which is present, to that which is immediately evidenced to us in inner and outer experience. It holds to fact and reality against that which is merely ideal, and it can recognise the ideal only when it presents itself as the deeper fact.

In all this the modern spirit withdraws itself from the Middle Ages, and claims kindred with antiquity. Yet it is impossible any longer to regard the modern movement of thought as merely a return to the light of ancient culture out of the *Dark Ages*. The long mediæval struggle of humanity for deliverance from itself cannot be regarded as simply a contest with spectres of its own raising, but must be taken as an essential stage in the progress of human thought. If the endeavour to crush nature under the dominion of spirit was in a sense irrational and fruitless, seeing that it is only *in* nature that spirit can be revealed, yet that endeavour has for ever made impossible the easy reconciliation of the two with which the ancients were satisfied. A mere return to antiquity must produce, as it always has produced, a culture which falls below that of antiquity both in fulness and depth. For the ancient civilization was not impoverished, as such a revival of it must be, by ignoring problems which had not yet been opened up. As Goethe found his idea of Iphigenia most fully realised in a Christian saint,[1] so we may say that the perfect form of Greek art cannot be again

[1] *Italienische Reise*, Oct. 19, 1786.

reproduced except by a spirit which has passed through the Christian *Sanctuary of Sorrow*.

On the other hand, if the moderns can return to the ideals of the Middle Ages, it is on a higher level, at which such ideals no longer come into conflict with the naturalistic spirit of antiquity. In like manner the secular scientific impulse, which, in the last century, was working towards an altogether mechanical and external explanation of the world, begins, with Goethe himself, to bring back in a higher sense, under the names of organism and development, that explanation of the world by final causes, which in a lower sense it has rejected. And the vain attempts still made to explain spirit by nature are rapidly teaching us to revive the truth which underlay the mediæval supernaturalism, that in the last resort nature is only to be explained by spirit.   Perhaps it may be found that no one has done more to prepare the way for such a reunion of ancient and mediæval ideas than our great modern poet and prophet of the religion of nature, Goethe.

ROUSSEAU

The Reaction against Rousseau's Influence—His *Confessions*—Opposition of the Inner to the Outer Life—His Education—His "Effeminate and Indomitable Character" —His Ideal—Effect of Parisian Life upon him—His Literary Labours and their Effect upon him—The *Causes of Inequality*—The *Social Contract*—The *Emile*—Contradictions in his View of the Influence of Social Life upon the Individual—His Individualism in Politics—His Theory of Education—His Idea of Religion—The *Raison Commune* and the *Volonté Générale*—False Tendency to Abstraction and Simplification—The Natural Man—The Reformation and the Revolution.

ROUSSEAU is one of those authors whom we can never afford wholly to forget. His value indeed does not consist in any consummate literary achievement : for he is too much of a prophet to be ever completely successful as an artist. That persistent reiteration of certain ideas, that perpetual insistence upon certain modes of feeling, which was the condition of his power over his own generation, makes him often tedious, and sometimes, it must be confessed, even nauseous to readers of the present time, in spite of the point and dignity and riches of his utterance. Just because he spoke to such willing and attentive ears in his own time, ours are now shut against him. Like his Julia, we have " drunk the sweet and bitter cup of sensibility to the lees," and the *Nouvelle Héloïse*, with its fruitless self-analysing ecstasy of feeling, can no longer tempt us. If the reign of Puritanism has all but taken all meaning and reality out of the Scriptural language of the Protestant Reformers, it is not wonderful that Robespierre and St. Just with their many followers have made the cant of

abstract patriotism and natural right intolerable to
us. And the sentimental Deism of the Savoyard
vicar has long been recognised both by believers
and unbelievers to have too little substance, too
little definiteness and concrete meaning, to make
a religion. In art and politics, in philosophy and
theology, we have outgrown, at least we have
ceased to relish, the abstract Gospel of subjective
feeling and individual right, and we can no longer
revive in its original intensity the charm which it
had for those to whom it was first addressed.

Yet without a study of Rousseau and his contemporaries, it is impossible for us to understand
ourselves, or the great change which has taken
place in human thought within the last century.
Rousseau is the " short abstract and chronicle of
his time." The tragedy of revolution, which was
necessary to the new birth of European civilisation, was enacted in his breast ere it passed on to
the stage of history. In his *Confessions*, and many
vindications of himself, with their mad self-exalta-
tion and self-exposure, their deification of the
individual Ego, which is yet at the same time
shown in all its naked meanness and littleness, we
have the diseased spirit of the time gathered to a
focus of intensity in which all its contradiction is
clearly displayed. The infinite ambition combined
with the sordid reality of Rousseau's life, his con-

fident and yet impotent aspiration after better forms of social union, both in the family and the state, combined with his utter incapacity for establishing healthy relations with one single human being, his constant reiteration of good wishes and intentions, and his persistent claim that the will should be taken for the deed, combined with the ever-reviving consciousness that the will is not the deed, and the desire to thrust upon society the responsibility of his own failure—all this forms a picture of complicated mental agony which we can scarcely bear to contemplate, except as a phase of the *Welt-Schmerz*, which is the condition of progress. The easy external interpretation has often been given that Rousseau was maddened with vanity, and that even his flight from the world was an effort to attract its notice. But, as Mr. Morley says in his admirable biography, Rousseau's vanity, if it can be so called, "belonged to another sphere of motive" than any ordinary affectation of singularity.

The truth is, that he was so intensely occupied with the endless struggle with himself, the endless effort to find anodynes for his own self-dissatisfaction, that he could not possibly have cherished that care for the opinion of others, that common kind of vanity, which characterised so many of the literary men of his time. Rousseau lived in a world of his own phantasy, and in his later days at least, the world without was to him little more than an impersonal Greek chorus to the intense drama that was being enacted within his own soul. He had, indeed, a diseased desire to reveal himself, a diseased craving for the confirmation by others of his own judgment of himself; and failing of this confirmation, he turned bitterly away from the world as his enemy. But for the world's opinion in itself he had no such respect as would induce him either to hide anything from it, or to put anything but what he believed to be truth before it. Those who opposed, even those who interfered with him in any way, he seemed to identify with the accusing voices within him which he sought to silence. Thus suspicion grew to bitterness, and bitterness to isolation and madness, till, in his last work,—which, in spite of its monomania, is one of the most perfect expressions of a kind of melancholy peace found in the heart of despair itself,—he declares that not only the literary and ecclesiastical cliques with which he has quarrelled, not only the whole present, but all future generations, are and will be in a conspiracy to blacken his name and memory. The *Reveries* are the egoism of a broken heart, which even in breaking will not give up its egoism. But they are only the natural culmination of that "custom of nourishing himself on his own substance, and seeking all his pasture within himself," which was the bane of his whole life.

Rousseau was a son of the Swiss Republic of Geneva, and he remained long enough in his native city to receive an indelible impression from its religious and political traditions. Set to learn the business of engraving with a hard taskmaster, at the age of sixteen he escaped into Savoy, and to secure a welcome he became, or pretended to become, a convert to the Church of Rome. But his later works show that the practices of Catholic devotion never took any real hold of him, and that religion never was to him anything but a relation of the individual soul to God. In like manner, when at a later period he tried to formulate his conception of politics, he found it impossible to conceive liberty existing as under any more complex constitution than that of a Municipal State like Geneva.

More important, however, among the influences of Rousseau's youth than even Calvinistic religion and republican politics, was that unhealthy stimulation of sensuous and imaginative feeling which began in his earliest years, and finally reached a degree of passionate intensity beyond the limit of sanity. At the age of six he was already an eager reader of romances, and had learnt to waste himself in the luxury of passive emotion ; and the wandering, unsettled life on which he entered after his flight from Geneva, interrupted though it was by vehement but unmethodical fits of study in different directions, chiefly in music and literature, did nothing to restore the balance of his mind.

Gradually he developed a temper so made up of sensitiveness and impulsiveness, that it is scarcely possible to conceive a condition of life in which it could have preserved harmony with circumstances and with itself. " He has only *felt* during the whole course of his life," wrote Hume, after some intercourse with him, " and in this respect his sensibility rises to a pitch beyond what I have seen any example of : but it still gives him a more acute feeling of pain than of pleasure. He is like a man who was stripped not only of his clothes, but of his skin, and turned out in that situation to combat with the rude and boisterous elements." [1] And Rousseau's analysis of his own " effeminate but indomitable character " is very much to the same effect :—" In everything," he says, " gêne and subjection are insupportable to me, they would make me hate pleasure itself." [2] " In order to do good with pleasure, it is necessary for me to act freely, without restraint ; and to take away all the sweetness of a good work from me, it is only neces-

[1] Morley's *Rousseau*, ii. 299.   [2] *Confessions*, i. 5.

sary that it should become my duty." "Be it man or duty or even necessity that lays a command upon me, when my heart is silent, my will remains deaf, and I cannot obey ; I see an evil threatening me, but I let it come rather than agitate myself to prevent it. In every imaginable thing, what I cannot do with pleasure, it is impossible for me to do at all." [1]

To such a disposition the relations of society must be a constant irritation, because in its impulsive self-abandonment it is ever creating for itself obligations the weight of which it is unable to sustain, and also because it cannot understand any middle term between complete union and hostility. We do not therefore wonder to hear Rousseau saying, " I have never been fitted for civil society where all is gêne, obligation, and duty. My independent temper makes me incapable of the subjections necessary to him who would live with men."

The only social relation Rousseau could understand was that intimate communion of simple cares and pleasures, that continual easy expansion of heart, which can be found only in a narrow domestic circle, secured from the intrusion of all except those who are everything to each other. This Rousseau enjoyed, or thought he enjoyed,

[1] *Reveries,* vi.

for a short time in his youth in the household of
Madame de Warens, and his after-life was a continual regret and longing for the lost Paradise.
" Le vide," he once said, " de l'âge mûr, qui s'est
fait sentir à moi, me retrace le doux temps du
premier âge." The idea of a simple rustic life of
domestic peace, remote from all the noises of the
world, returns again and again in his works, and is
the source of their most beautiful passages. Connected with it is that love of the country, that
perfect delight in natural beauty, which made his
words a kind of revelation to a nation whose
cultivated classes had fled from the country and
were rapidly turning it into a desert. The pressure
of circumstances, however, and Rousseau's own
temper, soon put an end to the *Idyll of Les Char-
mettes*, and he was drawn by the necessity of his
vocation to Paris, the great centre of the intellectual life of the time.

Paris was to Rousseau an atmosphere of almost
fatal stimulation. It completed his literary education, and made him conscious of his powers. At
the same time, it threw him back upon himself
with a violent repulsion from all that he heard and
saw around him. A poor man, he had learned
the depth of the joys that are open to the poor,
and the temptations of a luxurious and artificial
life came too late even to touch him. Accustomed

to the simple and unrestrained life of the country, he was never at his ease in the brilliant and dissipated society in which he found himself. Rousseau could understand, in a measure, the ideal life with all its renunciations ; he could understand fully the simple delights of the senses and the affections. But the bright encounter of wit, the charm of social elegance, were to him as good as nothing ; and the literary and philosophic life of the time was worse than nothing. Both his lower and his higher nature made him long for a kind of plain living and high thinking, which was not to be found in the Paris of the eighteenth century. Above all, the sceptical temper of a society which was then sitting at the feet of Voltaire repelled and disgusted him. " I hate," he once said, " this rage to destroy without building up." [1]

It was the revolt of Rousseau's whole soul against the life and culture of Paris that gave such force and intensity to his denunciation of the evils of an artificial civilisation, and to his prophetic call to a perverse generation to return to nature. Forced back upon himself, he sought in his visions a compensation for his practical incapacity either to conform himself to the world, or the world to himself, and " while he was musing the fire burned." Rousseau, in fact, was rather like a

[1] *Mémoires de Mme. d'Epinay*, ii. 66.

Hebrew prophet under an ecstasy of inspiration than a literary man setting himself a definite task. Till near the age of forty he had thought of music rather than of literature as his vocation. He wrote his books under the weight of ideas that over-stimulated and over-mastered his weak sensibility, and forced his natural indolence for several years—" six years of madness and fever," he says —to the most strenuous tasks of literary composition. And when he had uttered his message he sank into a long silence, broken only by polemical or autobiographical writings. He always spoke of his literary career as his greatest misfortune ; and this, which was generally taken for affectation, was probably, in his sense, nothing more than the truth. The tension of thought and utterance once passed by, Rousseau found himself exhausted and unstrung, incapable any longer of the simple happiness which he always regarded as the best result of life. Between the ecstasy and almost agony of vision and expression, the excitement of literary success, and the persecutions by which it was followed, his sensitive mechanism had received a fatal shock. The world had come into his life, and, seek what solitude he would, he could no longer shut it out. He persisted, however, to the last in believing that he needed only one thing for the return of his former peace, namely, a complete exclusion of the world ; and the fact that peace would not return seemed to him a proof that the world was in a conspiracy against him. A frenzy of suspicion took possession of him, as of the Jacobins in the Reign of Terror, when the disappointment of their hopes of an unearthly Millennium seemed to be in itself a sufficient proof of the continued machinations of aristocrats.

There is, in truth, more than a superficial analogy between the two cases. The pure fanatical spirit of revolution which animated the Jacobin chiefs can awake in those, and in those only, who forget that we are always accomplices in the evils that oppress us, and who therefore set themselves to reform the world without an effort to reform themselves. Something more than the death of aristocrats, something after which we may trust it is now striving in a more hopeful way, was needed to make France free. Something more than passive good wishes, and freedom from outward hindrances, is needed to give inner harmony to the soul of man. But Rousseau always held to the principle that *in magnis voluisse sat est*, that good intentions are everything, and that, if they bear fruit in bad actions, it is the fault of circumstances, of social arrangements, and not in any degree of the individual himself. Hence that insane self-glorification which startles us at the

beginning of the *Confessions*, in which he heads
the undisguised record of his weaknesses with the
assertion that he is the best of men.   It is no more
than the truth that Rousseau had a stronger longing for ideal good, a deeper sympathy with the
poor and the oppressed, a keener feeling for natural
and moral beauty, than perhaps any writer of his
time.   It was unfortunate, however, that the lover
of virtue and humanity was incapable of enduring
the presence of men in the concrete, and that his
whole life was an insatiable craving for pleasurable
sensations.   " The laurels of mere wishing are
withered leaves that never have been green."

Let us not, however, be unjust to Rousseau.
His very incapacity for action, his weakness in the
practical world, combined with the passionate
intensity of his inner life, were the necessary conditions of his power.   Repelled by the mere " rage
to destroy without building up," which had taken
possession of even the better minds of his time,
he asked himself what were the sound elements
beneath that which was artificial and corrupt in the
dissolving social organisation around him.   And,
like Wordsworth, who directly or indirectly received many influences from him,[1] he found these

[1] The influence of Wordsworth's residence in France upon
the direction of his thoughts has perhaps not been sufficiently
considered.

healthy elements in the love of nature and the sympathies and duties of the family. He revealed to a sophisticated generation the primal charities, the first affections, out of which the purity and sweetness of life must spring. If there is sometimes a strained and artificial tone in his denunciation of artifice, if there is a tinge of impurity in his pictures of the pure life of nature, we must remember that his passionate revolt against the disease of society would scarcely have been possible, if he had not shared it. "They that are whole have no need of a physician."

Moreover, it was something to find among the great literary men of such a time one who so entirely identified himself not with the cultured few, but with the uncultured man. "C'est le peuple qui compose le genre humain : ce qui n'est pas peuple est si peu de chose, que ce n'est pas la peine de la compter." Rousseau's sympathy with the common people, his demand for them not of charity but of social justice, the irresistible force of his assertion of the claims of bare humanity not only to toleration and help but to respect and reverence, was a new note added to the moral harmonies of life, a new interpretation of the Christian law of brotherhood. If it led immediately to revolt and revolution, it also led *beyond* revolution to a better order of social and political life. It was something in an age of social privilege " to make poor men proud,"—conscious of themselves and of their dignity as men : nay, it was even necessary, if a higher social dignity can only be formed out of freer and more self-dependent units. Burke, the great theoretical antagonist of the Revolution, who alone at the time saw the fundamental error of its abstract principles, was blinded by his historic imagination, when he supposed that full justice had been done to their partial truth in the institutions which the Revolution had to destroy.

In Rousseau's summons to his generation to return to nature, there was, however, as in his own character, an almost inextricable mingling of true and false elements. The state of nature to which he would have men return is by no means a fixed and definite thing. It is, in fact, defined rather negatively than affirmatively, by opposition to the artificial state which civilisation has produced. It is the life of the country as opposed to the life of towns, the life of the family as opposed to the life of the State, the life of simple tastes and natural pleasures as opposed to the life of cultivated luxury. Where, as in the *Discourse on the Causes of Inequality*, he attempts to be precise in his definitions, it reduces itself to the life of the savage, who is no better than an animal except in his superior craft, and who is so far worse than some animals that he has no permanent social tendency.

But Rousseau has no sooner drawn this description of the state of nature in all its bareness, than he begins to modify his assertion of its desirableness. The preferable state, he allows, is not the pure state of nature, but a stage of human development somewhat beyond it, in which there is at least a certain settled order of the family. Here is to be found the " golden mean between the indolence of the primitive state and the petulant activity of our selfishness, and it must be the most happy and durable state." The picture set before us at the end of the *Nouvelle Héloïse* is an idealised reproduction of the order of domestic life in a simple society, combined with many of the aids of civilisation.

Again, in the *Social Contract*, the political union itself is admitted to bring compensations with it, which are more valuable than the independence it forces us to renounce. " The passage from the state of nature to the civil state," he declares, " produces in man a very remarkable change, in so far as it substitutes justice for instinct as the guide of his conduct, and gives to his actions a morality which was hitherto wanting to them. . . . Though by this change he deprives himself of many of his natural advantages, those he acquires in return are so great, his faculties are exercised and developed, his ideas are extended, his sentiments are ennobled, and his whole soul is elevated to such a degree that, if the abuses of his new condition did not often degrade him below that from which he has emerged, he would have cause to bless without ceasing the happy moment which for ever rescued him from it, and which, out of a stupid and unthinking animal, made him an intelligent being and a man." [1]

Lastly, in the *Emile*, after a slight reference to the state of nature which dispenses man from the necessity of any artificial education, Rousseau dedicates the rest of the book to the description of an elaborate training by which the blessings of culture are to be attained without any loss of the independence and simplicity of nature.

Rousseau, therefore, in practice, treats the state of nature and isolation which he supposes to have existed in the past, merely as a point of view from which he may recommend a certain line of progress in the future. On one occasion he even says, that it does not matter whether or not the state of nature has ever existed. "It is no easy enterprise to disentangle that which is original from that which is artificial in the actual state of man, and to make ourselves well acquainted with a state which no longer exists, *which perhaps never has existed,*

[1] *Contrat Social,* i. 8.

and which probably never will exist in the future, but of which, nevertheless, it is necessary to have just notions, in order to estimate aright our present state." [1] In other words, the natural state is an ideal involved in the nature of man, and of which we may discover the traces underneath all his changes, just as we may assert that the social contract is tacitly implied and recognised in every actual society, though " it may never have found formal expression " in any constitution whatever.[2]

In looking for this ideal, Rousseau's method is always determined by the individualistic prejudices of his time. In morals, in politics, and in religion alike, he goes back from the complex to the simple ; and for him, the simple is always the purely individual, the subject apart from the object, the man apart from society. He does not see that in this way he is gradually emptying consciousness of all its contents, and that of the abstract individual at which he must finally arrive, nothing can be said.

The first step in the path of this logic leads him to treat the social bond in all its forms as something secondary and artificial, something that may easily lead to a corruption or distortion of the natural goodness of man, or which can only be

[1] Preface to the *Treatise on the Causes of Inequality*.
[2] *Contrat Social,* i. 6.

prevented from doing so by the most elaborate expedients. The aim of politics, he holds, is to maintain the natural independence of the individual in spite of the social union ; the State is grounded, not in man's natural sociality (for he is not naturally social), but in an external necessity. In the increase of population a time comes when the " obstacles which are opposed to their preservation in a state of nature become too great for the forces which each individual can employ to maintain himself in that state.[1]   It then becomes necessary for men to combine, and the problem of politics is, to secure the advantages of combination without the loss of individual liberty, " to find a form of association which may defend and protect the person and property of each associate with the whole common force, and in which each one, while he unites himself to all, yet may obey none but himself, and remain as free as before."   And this problem can be solved only in a State in which every one exercises the sovereign legislative power for himself ; for only in such a State can there be a *volonté générale*, which does not represent any particular interest ; only in such a State will the particular interests neutralise each other, so as to allow the general interest to come into force.   But on the other hand, a will, which is merely the

[1] *Contrat Social*, i. 6.

common element of all particular wills, cannot be in collision with any one of them ; and under its rule, therefore, every citizen may preserve his natural liberty.

In the *Emile* Rousseau's logic follows a similar course. The method of education, he constantly tells us, should be *negative* and not *positive*. " The greatest, the most important, the most useful rule of all education is not to gain time, but to lose it," *i.e.*, to guard the pupil against extraneous influences that anticipate the natural development of his power,—to keep the way clear, and then to stand aside, and let Nature do her work. The master is never to teach, but always to contrive that the pupil should discover everything for himself, never to constrain or command, but always leave the pupil to the teaching of experience. It is true, as Rousseau confesses, that this method really involves the most elaborate and artificial adaptation of circumstances that may influence the pupil in any way desired ; but this artifice is necessary, just because nature has been so much distorted by social arrangements. The aim of education is only to restore artificially the natural order of human development.

Now it is scarcely necessary to show that the idea which Rousseau is pursuing is an empty abstraction ; Rousseau himself practically confesses that it is so. To protect the natural man from all interference, to make society into a means, not of coercing or restraining the natural will, but simply of re-enforcing it, would, if it were possible, be to stop at the very outset the moral education of man. The untameable savage, just so far as he is untameable, is incapable of civilisation, and even slavery has sometimes been an instrument in the development of man's higher nature, by breaking down the arbitrariness of the undisciplined will. When Rousseau seeks to arrange education so that the child shall never feel the pressure of a will superior to its own, he is really doing all he can to prevent the growth of a moral consciousness.

The theory of the *Emile* might have its value—nay, it undoubtedly had its value—as a protest against a system partly ascetic and partly conventional, in which the natural tendencies of youth were neglected, or crushed under arbitrary routine ; but it leaves out of account the truth that man must die to live, must rise above himself in order to be himself, must have the caprice of nature subdued in him in order that he may attain to true freedom. Rousseau tries systematically to evade this necessity, to make the natural expand gradually into the moral, the selfish into the social, without a break or division between the higher and lower self ; yet even his own imperfect analysis of the social bond, and of the process of education, forces from him many admissions which are inconsistent with his theory.

The social pact, *e.g.*, is supposed to be based on the fact that there is a common element in all wills, a common interest of all the citizens, which therefore they may co-operate in pursuing, without prejudice to their particular interests. But Rousseau soon admits that the *volonté générale* is not the same as the *volonté de tous*, and that to maintain the social bond the former must subordinate, and even suppress the latter. Society must " force the individuals to be free," because their natural will, " the impulse of appetite, is slavery, and obedience to self-prescribed law alone is liberty." Thus, at a turn of the hand, the abstract individual passes into the abstract universal, and the anarchy of individual will changes into the despotism of the State. Starting with the idea of the natural independence of every individual, Rousseau ends with a social despotism, in which every interest of life is regulated and controlled by the State. And when in the *Emile* this contradiction is forced upon his attention, Rousseau thinks it enough to tell us that we must choose between the natural man and the citizen, for we cannot have both ; and that the defect of the present mode of education is that it is directed to two opposite ends, and therefore fails in attaining either, but only produces *hommes doubles*, who have neither the independence of the natural man, nor that absolute absorption in the *moi commun* of the State which characterised the citizens of ancient Rome or Sparta. Of any union of social and individual liberty which does not involve the suppression of one or the other, of any organic unity of society in which the freedom of the members shall be consistent with the unity of the body politic, Rousseau has no conception, and, just because of this, his theory fluctuates between one and the other. In the end he seems to despair of political life, and he seeks to educate his Emile independently of any society, or at least of any society beyond the family. The "sole natural education is the domestic education," and, when it is completed, the ideal pupil has learned to regard his civic duty as something secondary and accidental, and not as the real object of his life. Though, therefore, Rousseau makes the inconsistent admission that man is "sociable by his nature, or, at least, made to become so," and that the "civil state alone gives man that moral liberty which makes him truly master of himself," yet he never frees himself from the fixed idea of his individualism, that the natural man is good in himself, and that all the responsibility of his errors and perversions is to be thrown upon society.

The side of Rousseau's speculation which perhaps has best preserved its interest for the present time is his defence of religion.   In this defence he follows his usual method.   As he sought for the healthy elements of social life by abstracting from all the complexities of civilisation and falling back upon the sentiments of the natural man, so, beneath the various structures of dogma and institution in which the different religions of the world have realised themselves, he endeavours to distinguish the primitive movement of religious feeling.   As the State has its origin in a *moi commun* which is identical in all individuals, so religion must rest on a universal *sentiment intérieur*, a " conscience " or " common reason " (for Rousseau uses all these names for it), which is the residuum that remains when we leave out the differences of individuals and nations.   " I know," he says on one occasion, " that the common reason is very limited, and that, when we go beyond its narrow bounds, every one has his own reason that is proper to himself." This common reason teaches us to regard the world as a moral system whose centre is in God.   " The good man " obeying it " arranges all things with respect to the good of the whole ; the bad man " disobeying it " arranges the whole universe with respect to himself.   The latter makes himself the centre of all things ; the former measures his

radius, and keeps himself in the circumference.
Thus he finds his due place at once in regard to
the common centre, which is God, and in regard
to all the concentric circles, which are his fellow-
creatures." [1] The answer to all the objections of
pessimism, based on the existence of moral and
physical evil in the world, is ultimately to be found
only in the *sentiment intérieur* which teaches us
that God is, and that He is the maintainer of this
moral order in the universe. "We do not prove
the existence of God by the system of Pope, but
we prove the system of Pope by the existence of
God." Apart from this faith, all arguments for
either optimism or pessimism are a vain jangle of
words. For if the pessimists can point to the evils
visible in that small part of the universe which is
within our experience, it is always open to their
opponents to allege that these evils are necessary
to the attainment of the highest good, and that
they would disappear on a view of the whole. The
optimist "does not say that every single thing in
itself is good, but only that the whole is good, or
that all is good for the whole"; and "no one can
give direct proofs for or against this proposition,
for such proof could be derived only from a perfect
knowledge of the world and of the end proposed

[1] *Confession of a Savoyard Vicar;* cf. *Letter of Voltaire* on
Optimism.

by its author, a knowledge which incontestably is far above the reach of man." " If God exists, He is perfect ; if He is perfect, He is wise, almighty, and just ; if He is just and almighty, my soul is immortal ; if my soul is immortal, thirty years of life are nothing to me, and these years, with all that happens in them, may be necessary for the maintenance of the universe." If the first proposition is admitted, the rest can never be shaken ; if it be denied, there is no use in disputing about its consequences. Everything, therefore, depends on the truth of that inner sentiment which constrains us to believe in God. " I believe in God as fully as I believe in any other truth, because to believe or not to believe are the things in the world that are least under my control ; because when my reason is wavering, my faith cannot long rest in suspense ; because, finally, a thousand motives of preference attract me to the side that is most consoling, and join the weight of hope to the equilibrium of reason."

Have we then a right to believe whatever is " most consoling," whatever, in short, we most strongly desire to believe? Rousseau is fully aware of this objection to such an assertion of the rights of pure subjective feeling, but his only answer is that we must distinguish the mere feeling of the individual as such, from feeling as the utterance of the *raison commune*. " You bid me," he writes to one correspondent, " distrust this internal assent, but I find in it a natural safeguard against the sophisms of my understanding. And I fear that on this occasion you are confusing the secret inclinations of our heart which lead us astray with that more secret, more inward voice, which reclaims and murmurs against these interested decisions, and brings us back, in spite of ourselves, to the way of truth." At the same time, Rousseau confesses freely that this appeal to sentiment is powerless as an argument against those who say that they do not feel it. " A proof of sentiment for us," he allows, "cannot become a demonstration for them, and it is not reasonable to say to any one, ' You ought to believe this because I believe it.' " Rousseau is in the difficulty of one who appeals solely to the individual as such, who indeed admits no other appeal, and who nevertheless asserts that there is such a thing as universal truth. But, from this point of view, a universal truth could only be that which was believed by every one, *quod semper*, *quod ubique*, *quod ab omnibus* ; and the first man who honestly denied that he had any such conviction would seem to be a conclusive negative instance against its existence.

The truth is that Rousseau represents in its ultimate one-sidedness the principle of Protestantism.

Like Rousseau, Luther and Calvin appealed to the inner light, the immediate witness of the spirit, denying the right of the Church to stand between the individual and God ; like Rousseau, they declared that the only good evidence of religion is to be found in the inner experience of the believer. It is true that an attempt was made, especially by the second generation of Protestants, to put the Bible into the vacant place of the Church ; but the Bible was no self-interpreting authority, and the true interpretation of it was to be discovered by each one for himself. The spiritual man, the individual who had deepest Christian experience, was to judge all things, and no one would claim to overrule his judgment.

But this brings us back to the difficulty of which we have just spoken. When Rousseau asserted that there was a *raison commune*, whose voice was distinct from the voice of the individual understanding, a *volonté générale*, which was not to be confused with the will of any particular person, he was obliged at the same time to allow that we cannot be sure that this universal element in the intelligence and will of man is uttering itself in any one case or individual. For he admitted, not only that there is an early period in the life of the individual and the race, in which religion and morality can hardly be said to exist ; but also that even in later times it requires special conditions to maintain in the individual that purity and sincerity of heart by which the inner voice of nature can be clearly distinguished from the dictates of the natural will and the individual understanding. And in like manner, the Protestant assertion of the right, or rather of the duty, of private judgment, had to be interpreted as meaning, not that every one was a judge of moral and religious truth, but that every one could become capable of judging, by passing through the necessary spiritual experience. The spiritual man alone, therefore, was the judge of all things ; but who was the spiritual man? The question was one of subjective determination, and could as little be brought to any universal tribunal, as the corresponding question of Rousseau, who is the natural man? As in the former case, the spiritual man is needed to discover the spiritual man, so in the latter case the natural man is needed to find out the natural man.

The first effect of the Protestant appeal to the inner witness of the spirit was to awaken a thousand jarring and contradictory voices on every point of Christian doctrine. As it was admitted that every individual could be the organ of the spirit, so every founder of a sect expressed his own convictions as the Spirit's voice ; and Bossuet was soon able to point to the thousand variations of Protestants as the natural and necessary result of their appeal to the individual in place of the Church.

On the other hand, a growing sense of the difficulty of securing agreement led among the Protestants themselves to a more or less definite attempt to simplify the doctrine of Christianity. When divisions arise, the natural tendency of many minds is to fall back on the points which division has not yet touched, and to treat the matters in dispute as of little consequence. Christianity, it was argued, is something which every one must receive on the witness of his own spirit ; it must therefore be something free from difficulty and dispute, which the simplest can be expected so to receive. Hence we may abandon as extraneous to Christianity all those doctrines which are beyond the reach of the ordinary understanding. Even the most orthodox felt the force of this logic, and were led by it to throw into the background those doctrines which relate to the absolute nature of God, and to attach all importance to those which relate to his relations to man. And the most extreme of the Protestant sects, like the Moravians and Quakers, treated all objective doctrine whatever as a secondary affair, and concentrated their attention upon the analysis of the subjective religious experience of the individual.

Rousseau's *Profession of Faith of a Savoyard Vicar* is only the ultimate expression of this tendency. To decide fairly, the vicar argues, between the conflicting claims of the many competing religions of the world, or even between the many interpretations of Christianity, a man must spend his life in travel and research, must make himself a profound metaphysician and a thorough historian ; must combine the widest knowledge of facts with superhuman wisdom and insight. " *Je n'ai jamais pu croire que Dieu m'ordonnât, sur peine de l'enfer, d'être si savant.*" " How could Jesus Christ venture to promise the kingdom of heaven to the simple, and commence his most beautiful discourse by blessing the poor in spirit, if it requires so much wit to understand His doctrines?" The creed to which the heart witnesses is something simpler ; it reduces itself to the belief in an *Être Suprême*, who rewards the good and punishes the evil, and to whom therefore we ascribe the attributes of *wisdom* and *goodness*, though sensible that even these words express ideas of human excellence which, strictly speaking, are not transferable to the Divine Being. This alone is a creed which needs no extraneous authority of the Church, no evidence of a revelation given to some one else at a distant time, to accredit it, for it " depends on general principles common to all men," and every simple heart can verify it for itself. "*Est-il simple, est-il naturel que Dieu ait été chercher Moïse pour parler à Jean-Jacques Rousseau?*" [1]

The main difficulty in relation to this *Profession of Faith* has already been indicated. Rousseau is obliged to admit that the so-called universal belief is not universal ; that even this last residuum of religion is accepted only by those whose hearts are prepared for it. Hence his intellectual position was immediately out-flanked by those who still further simplified the dictates of the *raison commune*, and reduced them to morality without religion, or even, as was the case with some of those who were most possessed with the rage of simplification and negation, to the simple appetites.

Rousseau himself, in the description of the earliest state of the natural man, had indicated this necessary result of his logic,—a result from which, however, he had immediately recoiled. The search for universal truth as the simple, the natural, as that which commends itself at once to every individual, is suicidal, for in this search we are gradually forced to abstract the individual from all the conditions under which the universal power

[1] Letter to M. de Beaumont ; cf. the second Letter from the Mountain.

of reason can be manifested in him. To seek for the simple voice of nature in this way is about as reasonable as the experiment of the king who shut up an infant in a room by himself in order to determine the primeval language. If, as Rousseau says, " the man who reflects is a depraved animal," where shall we find the simple voice of reason, the unsophisticated utterance of nature? Only it would seem in the pure animal, the nature that feels and desires without reflection. Unfortunately the pure animal has no voice and no utterance whatever.

The great error of Rousseau was to seek the universal truth of religion in some abstract residuum, strained from all the various beliefs of men ; just as it was his great error in politics to seek the *volonté générale* in some element of agreement amid the jarring wills of all the citizens. There is no such element in either case. If there is a *raison commune* in the religious history of men, it must be sought in a universal spirit, which progressively manifests itself in and through the particulars as the unity that subordinates their difference and conflict, and not in the abstraction of an *Être Suprême*, which avoids all difficulties simply because it has no contents whatever.

Deism, as it appears in Voltaire and Rousseau, is not a religion at all. Its God is simply, to use a modern illustration, "a not-ourselves, that makes for righteousness," an external Being who attaches happiness to goodness, or a name for the supposed connection of the two, not a Spirit who transcends and embraces all things and beings, and works through the free life of spirits, even through their error and their sin, that he may bring them all to himself. Mr. Morley justly remarks that Deism is a "faith of egoism and complacency, a kind of gratuitously adopted superfluity, not the satisfaction of a profound inner craving and resistless spiritual necessity." Its inadequate conception of human freedom as a mere "liberty of indifference," divorcing man from God, and consequently also man from man, makes religion in the true sense of the word an impossibility, though it may still leave place for a feeling of moral aspiration. Optimist too as Rousseau was, he never once tasted the sweetness or felt the power of the religion of pity and reconciliation; and he divides the wicked from the good, and discusses the fate of each, without a sense of the brotherhood and solidarity of men." [1]

The work of the Revivers of learning and the Reformers, of the Encyclopædists and of Rousseau himself, was to assert the rights of reason; to assert, in other words, that the principle of all

[1] Morley's *Rousseau*, ii. p. 269.

man's knowledge and action is within him. Hence they were naturally led to oppose the inward to the outward, the witness of the spirit to the dead letter of tradition, private judgment to the authority of the Church. Such an assertion of the rights of the individual was necessary, if the implicit reason of faith and feeling was ever to become the explicit reason of science ; if the simple unreflected unity of the spirit with the doctrines and institutions of the Christian Church was ever to be mediated by reflection and consciousness.

And it must be remembered that this change of the form of religious thought involved also a great change of the matter ; for in becoming, what it essentially is, a religion of spirit, Christianity must necessarily learn to dispense with that machinery of external sign and symbol, of authoritative revelation and miraculous interference, which has been the support of its childhood. As in politics it is the problem of modern times to reassert the principle of order, the *volonté générale*, without the aid of that fiction of divine right—vested in kings or nobles, and separating them from all other men—which had been its inadequate expression in earlier days ; so in religion it is the problem of modern times to reassert the self-revelation of the divine spirit *in* the world, and *in* and *for* man, while erasing the absolute line of division with which previous ages had separated priest, and prophet, and apostle from those to whom they spoke.

But the difficulty lies in the transition. Thought develops slowly, and each generation is disposed to exaggerate even to absurdity the aspect of truth which is revealed to it. The Reformers were naturally led to lay too much emphasis on the change of the form of religion, and to give too little thought to the necessary reconstruction of its matter. Not discerning that the individual consciousness is what it is by means of the historical mediation through which it has passed, and that the Catholic Church itself was the necessary presupposition of Protestantism, they spoke as if the long labour of the middle ages had been for naught, and as if the one thing necessary was to sweep its accumulated results away, and go back to the simplicities of the first Christian faith. And it was by a kind of logical necessity—that logical necessity by which one-sided opinions disprove themselves and pass away—that the French successors of the Reformers sought to go back still further, from Christianity to heathen virtue, and from heathen virtue to the simple consciousness of the natural man. " The rage to destroy without rebuilding," which possessed the most extreme followers of Voltaire, is the necessary culmination of that assertion of the freedom of a merely formal reason against all the contents with which history has filled it. But to liberate man is not merely to break his chains.

The ultimate hope of the human spirit must be to restore as reason what it then sought to destroy as the unreason of authority, to restore as the realisation of freedom what it then rejected as the bonds of an external necessity. This restoration involves, as has already been said, a thorough *re-formation* (in the etymological sense of the word) of the whole edifice of dogma and institution in a way which few of the friends of religion have yet realised, and still fewer have had the faith and courage to attempt. Rousseau, with his instinctive revolt and repulsion at once against the philosophers of his time who sought merely to destroy the existing order, and against the priests who sought merely to resist its destruction, with his divided life, alternating between the fervid assertion of the principle of individualism in its extremest form—the glorification of the natural man—and his equally fervid assertion of the rights of the common reason and the general will, may be regarded as a *vox clamantis in deserto* to make straight the ways for a faith which is at one with reason.

WORDSWORTH

How he Repels and Attracts—Advantages of a Chrono-
logical Arrangement of his Poems—His View of the
Functions of Poetry—His Poetic Excellence and his
Defects—His Views as to Poetic Diction—Effect of the
French Revolution upon him—His Political Changes—
His Relations to Rousseau—His "Return to Nature"—
His Poetry of Nature—His Democratic Sentiment and
Poetry of Humble Life—His Faith in Man—His
Patriotism—His Autobiography in the Prelude.

It is to be hoped that the well-chosen selection of Wordsworth's poems which has been edited by Mr. Arnold may do something to extend the knowledge of his characteristic excellences. Wordsworth's poetry, indeed, can never become popular. It is like a pure fountain of living water, hidden away from the trodden paths of literature. To those who seek in poetry only the idealised echo of common passions, it must always appear cold and tasteless. It courts us with none of the usual subsidiary charms and illusions of verse ; and it requires, at first, something like a moral effort ere we can put ourselves into the temper for enjoying it ; " we must love it, ere to us it will seem worthy of our love." It requires us, in a sense, to become as little children, to divest ourselves of all artificial associations and secondary interests, of all that hides the essentials of humanity, and to enter a region where everything is estimated at the price which it has for the simplest and most universal human affections.

On the other hand, to those who can bear the

shock of this reversal of the usual standards of judgment, and can overcome the first recoil of the " natural man " from the outward sternness and plainness of Wordsworth, and the feeling of incongruity, or even absurdity, which is occasionally produced by his insensibility or indifference to ordinary associations, his poetry will be a source of that highest poetic pleasure which accompanies a deeper sense of the harmony of the world with the soul of man. It will be a kind of religious retreat from the jarring and inconsistency of things, in which they can renew their faith in the ultimate coincidence of " truth and poetry."

Wordsworth cannot be made popular. But one thing more might be done to give fair play to his " elective affinities," and to remove the increasing difficulties of understanding him, which time brings with it ; his poems might be rearranged in chronological order, and each of them might be accompanied with an explanation of the circumstances of its composition. Wordsworth is a poet, whose poetry gathers closely about his life, and cannot in many cases be fully appreciated except by those who carry in their minds some picture of the occasions when it was produced. From this point of view the present arrangement of the poems is altogether misleading and artificial— depending mainly on some psychological view of the relations of the different faculties, fancy, imagination, the affections, etc.—a view which is not very distinct, and which, at best, is foreign to the real interest of poetry. Nor would Mr. Arnold's arrangement of the poems as ballad, lyric, elegiac, etc., be much of an improvement as applied to the whole of the poems—however fitting it may be for a selection. The reader of poetry does not want illustrations either of abstract psychology or of the philosophy of Art ; the only thing he need care for—beyond the individual poems themselves —is the connection they have as different expressions of the same poetic spirit. And this, in the case of Wordsworth at least, he must care for, if he would fully understand their meaning. Anyone who will take the trouble to read the poems in the order in which they are mentioned in the *Life of Wordsworth*, and with the explanations there given, will at once feel this. Wordsworth's biographer truly says, that " the poems, to be studied profitably, should be read chronologically"; and Professor Knight, in his interesting volume on *The English Lake District as interpreted in the Poems of Wordsworth* (preface, p. 21), has urged the necessity of an edition such as we have described. We hope that, before long, Professor Knight, or someone equally competent, if such can be found, may be induced to undertake the

labour of such an edition.[1]   In that case, all that
is possible will have been done to remove outward
hindrances to the appreciation of Wordsworth,
and it may safely be left to time, to raise to his
proper place a poet whose fame depends so little
upon temporary or accidental attractions, and so
much upon the deepest and most permanent
sources of human emotion.

> If thou, indeed, derive thy light from heaven,
> Then, to the measure of that heaven-born light,
> Shine, poet, in thy place, and be content!

Wordsworth was a poet who took his vocation
in earnest.   He rejected as insincere " poetic
diction " the old invocations of the Muse ; but
no poet ever had a deeper sense of being a " dedicated spirit," a *vates sacer*, whose inspiration did
not come from himself.   He was for himself
prophet as well as poet, one whose vocation was
not merely to please men, but to teach them with
what they should be pleased.   " Every great
poet," he says, " is a teacher.   I wish to be considered either as a teacher, or as nothing."   When
the critics of his day reminded him that the end
of verse is to produce pleasure, he answered that
an original poet has to *create* the taste by which
he can be enjoyed.   " Of genius in the fine arts

[1] This passage was written before Professor Knight's classical
edition of Wordsworth's poems was published.

the only infallible sign is the *widening* of the sphere of human sensibility "; " genius is the introduction of a new element into the intellectual universe." And he met the neglect and ridicule, with which for many years his poetry was treated, with an unshaken faith that it was founded upon the truth of nature, and that it could not but find or make its audience.

Nor did this conviction relate only to form of expression, it related also to the content or matter expressed ; indeed the one could not be separated from the other. Wordsworth believed that he had a fresh and hitherto unexpressed view of man and his relations to the world to communicate, although he recognised that it is not the function of the poet to deal with truth directly, but only as it can find sensuous expression in beauty, and be made part of the emotional life of man. " The man of science seeks truth as a remote and unknown benefactor, he cherishes it and loves it in his solitude ; the poet, singing a song in which all human beings join with him, rejoices in the presence of truth as our visible friend and hourly companion. Poetry is the breath and finer spirit of all knowledge ; it is the impassioned expression which is on the countenance of all science." Wherever, in fact, science ceases to be a merely external thing ; wherever its isolated truths are brought together in relation to humanity, and are thus made part of our immediate consciousness of ourselves, they become, in Wordsworth's view, capable of poetic treatment. " Poetry is the first and last of all knowledge." If the time should ever come, when what is called science, thus familiarised to man, should be ready to put on a form of flesh and blood, the poet will lend his divine spirit to aid the transfiguration." Wordsworth thus makes poetry the counterpart and coadjutor of philosophy, in so far as it is the business of philosophy, by a last synthesis, to bring the manifold truths of science into unity with each other, and with the mind of man.

There are many critics at the present day who tell us that such a view of the office of the poet is altogether erroneous, and that poetry has nothing to do with the teaching of truth, or with truth in any shape. Some go so far as to say, that what we have to regard in a poet is not what he has said, but simply how he has said it. It is probably by way of protest against such a doctrine, that Mr. Arnold has allowed himself to say that " poetry is essentially a criticism of life " ; which it is, only in the same sense in which there *is* " a moral shut in the blossom of a rose," or in which a good man may be said to be a living criticism upon a bad one.

For it cannot be denied that, in poetry, the form is the first thing. *Its* function is pure expression for its own sake, and the consideration of what is expressed must be secondary. The Muses would undoubtedly prefer a good bacchanalian song to Zachary Boyd's metrical version of the *Bible*. Yet, after all, we cannot reckon it a great poetic advancement to write the best possible drinking song. Perfect, or relatively perfect, expression being given, we must ask what is expressed, and we cannot give the name of sacred poet to the " idle singer of an empty day," but only to him who can express the deepest and widest interests of human life ; nay, only to him who is in sympathy with the progressive movement of mankind, and who can reveal to us new sources of thought and feeling that have not before been touched. The only poetry that, in the long run, " humanity will not willingly let die," is that which contains not mere variations on the old themes, but " things unattempted yet in prose or rhyme."

Now Wordsworth can stand this test as well as any poet who ever lived. There is no poet who is more distinctly unique and of his own kind, no poet the annihilation of whose works would more obviously deprive us of a definite and original vein of thought and sentiment. And there is no poet, below the great master-lights of poetry, Homer, Shakespeare, Dante, and Goethe, whose work is so independent of theirs. Out of Goethe one might carve the materials for most of the modern poets of the second rank : but neither out of Goethe nor anyone else could one carve the materials for Wordsworth. And when Wordsworth is at his best, he stands quite on the level of the very highest.

After saying so much, we are bound to add that Wordsworth is often not at his best—that there is a defect in his utterance which distinctly separates him from the greatest poets, and which at times depresses him below even the second rank. His inspiration is lacking in continuity, and he is apparently unable to distinguish when he is inspired and when he is not. He feeds us at one time with angel's food, with " star fire and immortal tears," and at another time with the homeliest bread-and-butter of moral commonplace. Such poems as *The Star-gazers* or the *Sonnet written near Dover*, show the abruptness with which he falls and rises, from prose to poetry, from poetry to prose. Sometimes we are tempted to think that he struck off a few lines in the first heat of vision, and afterwards coolly filled in the rest when the vision had departed.

Such shocks of transition we do not often meet

with even in second-rate poets : for, when poetic
inspiration fails, they generally have rhetorical
resources to help them over the difficulty. But
Wordsworth is almost entirely free from rhetoric :
he has no *callida junctura* to disguise the union
of the products of pure imagination with less
valuable materials. His poetry is sometimes like
a geological stratum, which has been partially
transformed by fire, but in which unchanged
masses of sand and pebbles are embedded. The
baldest matter of fact and the barest moral commonplace are in not a few of his poems put side
by side with " thoughts that breathe and words
that burn."

But even this defect of Wordsworth seems to
have a counterbalancing advantage. Just because
he makes no artificial effort to raise himself above
the level of prose, but only lets himself be raised
by the swelling tide of inspiration, there is a
genuineness, an authentic stamp of poetic insight
on his best work, which cannot be mistaken. One
proof of this is that, however often repeated, his
utterances never seem to become hackneyed.
There is nothing unreal or rhetorical in them to
spoil ; and gold when it is quite pure will not
rust. And this is the more remarkable that a tone
of majesty so often prevails in his best passages :
for majesty is of all tones that in which an element

of artificiality or false sentiment most easily betrays itself. The reason seems to be that Wordsworth always writes (as he tells us the poet should always write) " with his eye on the object." Unfortunately it is sometimes the eye of the mere observer which isolates the object observed from all others, not the eye of the poet which finds the whole in every part, and, so to speak, dissolves the immediate perception of separate facts in the unity of one animating idea. Hence the conscientious exactness and faithfulness which kills everything like rhetoric, sometimes also checks and kills the movement of poetic imagination. Thus, to take an example from the first passage that presents itself, in the beginning of the Dedication to the *Sonnets on the River Duddon* we find the following verse :—

> " The minstrels played their Christmas tune
> To-night between my cottage eaves :
> While, smitten by a lofty moon,
> The encircling laurels, thick with leaves,
> Gave back a rich and dazzling sheen
> That overpowered their natural green."

In the last line the resolute exactness of Wordsworth is no doubt seen, but the very carefulness with which he describes the appearance before him seems to take us away from the " synthetic mood " of poetry, in which the living spirit of the whole

must overpower and subordinate the distinct appreciation of the details.   Yet again—for the
defects of genius are strangely bound up with
its qualities—this *prosaic* exactness has for its
counterpart what we may call a *poetic* exactness
of mind ; a simple and direct grasp of the truth
which gives to Wordsworth's treatment of the
most subtle and evanescent of spiritual influences,
something of the precision of a scientific definition.
He writes with his eye always on the object, and
he describes what he sees " in worlds to which
the heaven of heavens is a veil," with the same
firmness of touch which he uses in dealing with
" some simpler matter of to-day."

The confusion just indicated between two kinds
of truth, the truth of poetic imagination, and
the truth of simple observation, seems to underlie
Wordsworth's æsthetic heresy : that poetry is not
distinct in kind from prose, and that " the language
of real life," as he calls it, when purified from
degrading or conventional elements, is at once
adapted for poetic uses.   In this his determination
to get rid of the meaningless " poetic diction,"
then in fashion, and to seek the poetic in the
natural, makes him forget the immense distinction
between the utterance which is an end in itself
and the utterance which is a means to an end.
As philosophers have said that the " real is the

rational," so a poet may be allowed to declare that
the "real is the poetic"; but this must not be
understood to mean that the world, as it is to
mere common sense and the ordinary understanding, is in itself poetic, but only that there is
nothing in the world which cannot *become* poetic,
if it is seen *sub specie æternitatis*, under the
"light that never was on land or sea." But
though Wordsworth sees that "the consecration
and the poet's dream" are needful, ere the world
can be what it is to the imaginative insight of
the poet; yet often, both in practice and theory,
he encourages the idea that there is no vital distinction between the prosaic and the poetic view
of the world, and therefore between the modes
of language in which each has to be expressed.

We cannot, however, fully appreciate the
strength and the weakness of Wordsworth, without looking beyond these formal considerations,
and asking what are the main ideas by which he
is guided and inspired, or, in other words, what
is the *content* of his poetry.

Wordsworth would probably have been willing
to accept it as a fair description of his work that
he had brought poetry back to nature. But this
only suggests another question—what did Wordsworth mean by *Nature*? The generation to which
he spoke was one to which the lesson "Return

to Nature " was preached by many voices, and with many shades of meaning. Indeed it might be said without much exaggeration that the whole labour of that generation, speculative and practical, was an effort to discover the true interpretation of that old maxim of the moralists. The boundless hope of the regeneration of man, of the liberation of his " nature " from the powers that oppressed it, and prevented its manifestation, which was expressed in different ways by Rousseau and by the Encyclopædists, found an echo in all civilised countries. And almost every youth who afterwards showed anything of the power of genius was swept away by the new enthusiasm of humanity that attended the first stages of the French Revolution.

> " Before them shone a glorious world,
> Fresh as a banner bright unfurled
>   To music suddenly."

> " Bliss was it in that dawn to be alive,
> But to be young was very heaven."

To such spirits the Revolution in its first dawn appeared to promise the absolute liberation of man from the yoke of custom and tradition, and to put the highest social good within his immediate grasp. They felt as men awakening from a charmed sleep, and the evils of the past were in their eyes like the creations of a troubled dream, which the daylight must for ever banish. It seemed to them for the time that the hindrances to human happiness were merely external, and that with the removal of a few corrupt institutions the social ideal could be at once realised. *Nature* was that sound kernel, that basis of truth and goodness in humanity, which would be reached at once by simply removing a few husks and excrescences which had overlaid and concealed it.

Of all those who felt the contagion of that enthusiasm of hope which prevailed in France in the dawn of the Revolution, no one was more deeply influenced by it than Wordsworth, for it appealed to thoughts and feelings which had been growing strong in him through all his earlier education among the Cumberland hills. It made him conscious of himself and of his vocation. Wordsworth, indeed, was never, so far as we know, a worshipper of Rousseau.[1] Indeed he never was one who learned much directly from books ; his reluctance to reading was at all times great, and in later years grew into positive aversion. But he was singularly responsive to the influences of outward nature, and also, at least during his youth and early manhood, he was deeply moved by the

[1] He quotes Rousseau only once, I think, in the *Epistle to the Bishop of Llandaff*.

spirit of the times in which he lived. As he paints
himself in the *Prelude*, we see that the one strong
power that moulded his early life was the " dear
native region " ; and he refers but doubtfully and
coldly to any other teacher. The simple, almost
rustic freedom of the life which he then lived in
the hills of Cumberland took so strong a hold
upon him that he never cared for any other. He
had Rousseau's distaste for what seemed to him
the luxurious and artificial life of cities.

> " The services of artificial life,
> And manners finely wrought, the delicate race
> Of colours lurking, gleaming, up and down,
> Through that state arras woven with silk and gold,
> . . . . I neither knew nor cared for."

Every high and pure feeling in him was, as he
tells us, associated with the life of shepherds.

> " Love had he found in huts where poor men lie,
> His daily teachers had been woods and rills,
> The silence that is in the starry sky,
> The sleep that is among the lonely hills."

The only effect of his stay at the University
of Cambridge seems to have been to drive him
back upon himself, and to make him feel that he
" was not for that hour, nor for that place." In
the *Prelude* his almost comic apologies for his
neglect of the studies of the University are

mingled with doubts whether it would have been
for his advantage to have attended to them.   And
before the natural term of college life was reached,
he had defied the censure of his friends, and
escaped with a chosen companion for a long walking tour in France, Italy, and Switzerland, which
supplied the subject for his earliest published
poem, the *Descriptive Sketches*.   But the joy of
France, then in the first enthusiasm of liberty,
took hold upon him, and he returned to that
country to watch for more than a year the course
of the Revolution—of which, indeed, he was in
some danger of becoming a victim if he had not
been recalled to England by his friends.   The
deep despondency, and almost despair, into which
he was thrown by the events of the Reign of
Terror, and still more by England's declaration
of war against the French Republic, are pictured
in his autobiographical poem, and also in his
account of " The Solitary," in the *Excursion*.
Living in the Isle of Wight, he tells us how his
heart sank within him as he listened every evening
to the cannon of the English fleet : he even confesses that he rejoiced in every defeat or disaster
of the English armies, and that he only became
reconciled to the war with France, when France
seemed to become a weapon of the ambition of
Napoleon.

After the French attack upon Switzerland, however, his sympathies changed, and even began to run with vehemence in another direction. France was now to him the great oppressor of the world ; and in some of his noblest verse he greeted every appearance of national resistance to the conqueror. In the remarkable pamphlet which he wrote against the Convention of Cintra, he denounced that Convention as showing on the part of the English generals an utter disregard of the moral forces arrayed against Napoleon. And in his fine sonnets *On National Liberty and Independence* he expresses his conviction that these forces are everything. " The power of armies is a visible thing, formal and circumscribed in time and space," and it cannot conquer the " subtle element," the irrepressible force of national life, which " rises like water."

> " Winds blow and waters roll,
> Strength to the brave, and power and deity,
> *Yet in themselves are nothing.*"

Wordsworth's political changes have been the subject of considerable comment. And it is true that in the somewhat narrow conservatism of his age we almost lose sight of the young enthusiast who rejoiced in the name of Republican. His later hostility to France he could, indeed, justify by saying that the same principles which led him to sympathise with the French when they were defending their liberties, made him turn against them when they became the enemies of national liberty in other countries. Yet this alone will scarcely carry us over the gulf that separates the disciple of Rousseau, who wrote the *Epistle to the Bishop of Llandaff* and the *Descriptive Sketches*, from the panegyrist of Laud and Charles the First, who wrote the *Sonnets on Ecclesiastical History*. The truth is, that Wordsworth's antagonism to the abstractions of revolutionary theory carried him ultimately, as it carried many at that time, dangerously near to the opposite extreme.

Besides, we must not expect too much of any human life ; and the flow of Wordsworth's inspiration began about the year 1816 to give place to the inevitable ebb. The struggle was over, and a repose, which was partly the repose of age, stole upon his mind. With a few notable exceptions, the products of his genius after this period are the imperfect echoes of the old music ; or, as in the case of the *Sonnets on Ecclesiastical History*, they are a kind of poetical exercises, which are rather a burden than an addition to his earlier works. One of the advantages of a chronological arrangement of the poems would be the separation of this feebler " aftermath " from the first rich harvest of the muse.

Leaving out of account this tribute to human weakness, however, there is a sense in which we may truly say that Wordsworth was faithful to the end to the principles of his youth ; or that the change through which he passed was only the change of a true development, the change of the acorn into the oak.   What made him in his youth so strong a partisan of the Revolution was his faith in man, and his indifference to all the external disparities of rank and circumstance ; and he was a believer to the last in this primitive gospel of liberty, equality, and fraternity. The apparent failure of the French Revolution, the gathering tragedy of the Reign of Terror, came to him, therefore, not merely as a painful shock of surprise and disappointment, but as a deadly blow at his faith in good and his hopes for humanity.

The way in which such a blow is met is a fair gauge of moral strength.   To the majority of the enthusiasts of the time the result of the Revolution in France brought nothing but the feeling that they had been the victims of an illusion ; nothing but a lesson of sceptical moderation and a loss of faith in spiritual forces.   There were others—and their successors still remain—who were unable either to give up their passionate hope for humanity or to change its form, and who persisted in repeating with increased vehemence the creed which destiny had weighed in the balance and found wanting. But in minds really creative and original, the disappointment gave occasion neither to despair nor to violence, but became a critical turning point of thought, leading them to ask how the belief in man which they could not surrender, was to be reconciled with the failure of their immediate expectations. For such minds, the ideas of " Nature " and " Liberty," the ideas of the Revolution, did not become unmeaning, but received a new interpretation, in which they were purified, as by fire, from the base alloy with which they had been mingled. An idea, like a seed, " cannot be quickened unless it die," and only those, who could keep the faith of the Revolution unquenched through its seeming failure, were capable of finding out the truth which underlay that faith and gave it its power.

Now, among the men of genius who sought thus to re-interpret the ideas of the time, the name of Wordsworth deserves a high place. If we contrast him with some of the greatest poetic voices of his generation, with Shelley or Byron, we see that while they on the whole belong to the Revolution, Wordsworth belongs to the Reconstruction. That stormy discontent with self and the world, which utters itself in every poem of Byron, contains little that had not been expressed with greater force by Rousseau, unless it be that Rousseau speaks the voice of hope, and Byron that of disappointment, if not of despair. And though the somewhat shrill, but pure and penetrating, melody of Shelley's song seems to be far removed from the sentimentalism of Rousseau, yet the essential purport of it is the deification of pure impulse, the vindication of nature as against all restraints.

On the other hand, Wordsworth's poetry is in its essence original and creative ; it carries us into a new intellectual region in which the ideas of the Revolution have not perished, but have, as it were, risen again in a better form. Of course, this does not at once settle the comparative value of Wordsworth's poetic achievements ; for the content of poetry is nothing without the form. But, on the other hand, it may be equally said that the form is little without the content ; and in the gift of creative insight, which makes him the poet of the future rather than of the past, Wordsworth stands beyond every poet of his day, except Goethe. And if he is without Goethe's wide culture and sympathy with all the elements of social and intellectual progress, he is, as unmistakably as Goethe himself, the representative of new spiritual forces, of thoughts and feelings which had never found poetic expression until Wordsworth expressed them.

That this is true, and that Wordsworth is a poet with whom the principles of the Revolution acquire a new and higher meaning, may be seen more clearly by a comparison of the leading ideas of his poetry with those of Rousseau. Rousseau, like Wordsworth, was the prophet of Nature, as opposed to everything that is arbitrary and conventional. And this general contrast had with him three different though closely related meanings.

In the first place, Rousseau called attention to certain harmonies between the outward world and the soul of man, which till his time had passed almost unobserved. He found outward Nature to be most human in its meaning, just where it had been hitherto regarded as most inhuman. Not the garden or the meadow, but the " sounding cataract, the tall rock, the mountain, and the deep and gloomy wood," were his chosen haunts. He reconciled man to the world, and taught him to find rest and refreshment for the weary spirit in the wild freedom of Nature, and in presence of those awful manifestations of her power which had hitherto been considered most alien and unfriendly to humanity. And in this way he opened up sources of emotional experience, springs of poetry and imaginative delight, which had scarcely been touched by any writer before his time.

Again, in the second place, Rousseau meant by

a *return to Nature*, an assertion of the supreme importance of the primary bonds of human affection, and in connection therewith, of the dignity of the humblest forms of human labour, and especially of the pastoral and agricultural life. A simple rustic existence, in which the charities of the family are little disturbed by the ambitions and rivalries of civilisation, seemed to him to be the ideal of what is healthful for man, morally and intellectually. Hence his denunciations of luxury, and his fanatical attack on the arts and sciences, as corrupting the simplicity of human life—extravagances which received a colour of excuse from the fact that they were addressed to a society in which the weapons of civilisation had been often turned against the first principles of social morality.

Lastly, Rousseau meant by a *return to Nature*, a return by each man upon himself, an awakening in him of a consciousness of his capacities, his rights, and his duties. The individual man was to him, not merely a part in a great social whole, but a whole in himself, a being not to be subjected to any *external* authority, to any authority except the *raison commune* which " lighteth every man that cometh into the world." In this sense the teaching of Rousseau was only a last development of the principle of the Reformation, that no authority can claim man's belief or homage, except the God who speaks within him. Unfortunately the doctrine was formulated by Rousseau in such a way as to sever the individual from that general social life of humanity, through which all spiritual culture must come to him ; and thus the vindication of freedom changed, in his hands, into a declamation against civilisation, and an apotheosis of the " noble savage."

Now it may be shown that almost all Wordsworth's most powerful and characteristic utterances grew out of one or other of these three lessons of Rousseau—though, at the same time, not one of them is simply echoed, but all are transformed in the light of a purer, if not a greater, genius. Wordsworth is Rousseau moralised, Christianised, and, as it were, transfigured by the light of imagination. The one-sidedness of the revolutionary ideas may not always be completely transcended ; but a deeper spiritual feeling, and a finer poetic insight, has done much to discover the essential truth of the gospel of " Nature and Freedom," and to separate it from the baser elements, with which in Rousseau it was mingled.

1. The love of the wilder and grander aspects of natural beauty, of mountain and woodland untouched by the hand of man, is the first element of Wordsworth's poetry. No one has expressed more fully the power of wild nature to elevate and

refresh the soul of man, to stir within him new sympathies, which are deeply seated, and, perhaps, for that very reason were long hidden from the ordinary consciousness. His first gift as a poet, the natural basis of his genius, was that intense organic sensibility to the immediate beauties of sight or sound, which showed itself even in his earliest years. " Yes," he says—

> " Yes, I remember when the changeful earth
> And twice five summers on my mind had stamped
> The features of the moving year, even then
> I held unconscious intercourse with beauty
> Old as creation, drinking in a pure
> Organic pleasure from the silver wreaths
> Of curling mist, or from the level plain
> Of waters, coloured by impending clouds."
>
> (Vol. v. 176.)

While in his boyhood, he had already noticed " the infinite variety of natural appearances which had not been mentioned by the poets, so far as I was acquainted with them." This natural sensibility of his was, as it were, the crystallising centre round which his poetry grew ; but it is seldom that in his verse he is content simply to picture the objects before him. His most common method is to make the immediate object the starting-point of a meditative thought which hovers between the outward and the inward, and

uses each alternately to interpret the other. His
great theme, as he tells us, is the " wedding "
of the intellect of man " to this goodly universe,
in love and holy passion." And somehow the
slow ruminative movement, with which he seeks
out the correspondence and harmonies of nature
and spirit, does not prove inconsistent with the
sensuous fervour of poetry. The poems on
Matthew, or the *Ode to Lycoris*, show how
Wordsworth can make meditation musical, without any heightening of its natural tones.

Perhaps, however, his greatest successes, those
in which he reaches the height of absolute vision,
are to be found in certain passages in which, by
a single stroke, he breaks down the wall between
outward and inward, so that " finding " and
" creating " seem to be only different aspects of
the same thing. One familiar instance of those
sudden and certain intuitions by which Wordsworth not seldom dissipates the veil of sense, and
brings us into unity with nature, may be given—
the passage about the boy on Windermere, who

" Blew mimic hootings to the silent owls
　That they might answer him ; and they would shout
　Across the watery vale and shout again
　Responsive to his call, with quivering peals
　And long halloos, and screams, and echoes loud
　Redoubled and redoubled ; concourse wild

Of jocund din. And when there came a pause
Of silence, such as baffled his best skill,
Then sometimes in that silence, while he hung
Loitering, *a gentle shock of mild surprise*
Has carried far into his heart the voice
Of mountain torrents ; or the visible scene
Would enter unawares into his mind,
With all its solemn imagery, its rocks,
Its woods, and that uncertain heaven received
Into the bosom of the steady lake."

Such passages—and many more remarkable might
be quoted—cannot be read without a " gentle
shock of mild surprise " at the coincidence or
correspondence of inward and outward, as at the
sudden appearance of a friend's face under a strange
disguise. By such electric strokes, even more than
by the direct expression of his poetic creed, though
that also is not wanting, Wordsworth makes us
feel that it is one spirit that speaks in man and
nature, and that, therefore, the poet's vision is no
mere playing with metaphors, but a real discovery
of " a presence far more deeply interfused." The
poet, with trembling and watchful sensibility,
seems to stand between the worlds, and catches the
faintest sounds of recognition that are carried from
one to the other.

" Hark ! it is the mountain echo,
Solitary, clear, profound,

Answering to the shouting cuckoo,
Giving to her sound for sound.
Such rebounds the inward ear
Catches sometimes from afar—
Listen, ponder, hold them dear,
For of God, of God they are."

Again, if for Wordsworth there is no absolute division between man and the material world, if for him " sun, moon, and stars all struggle in the toils of mortal sympathy," it was to be expected that his eye would be keen to detect the links of unity, the correspondences, that connect man more directly with living creatures. The daisy and the celandine, the broom and the thorn, are for him living friends and companions. To him " the meanest flower that blows can give thoughts that do often lie too deep for tears," though characteristically he speaks almost exclusively of the *wild* flowers, and he has little to say about the cultured beauties of the garden. And the same spirit makes him keen to detect and express the secret bonds of sympathy that grow up between man and the animals that stand nearest to him, especially the dog and the horse. The mystic charm of the *White Doe of Rylstone* lies in the way in which the doe, without transgressing the bounds of its natural life, is yet lifted up into the sphere of human sorrow and human sympathy. In *Peter*

Bell Wordsworth even tries—with partial success —to change the current of ordinary associations by making the ass the means of awaking the voice of humanity in the man.

2. This tendency of Wordsworth to " penetrate the lofty and the low," however, leads us to notice the second point of connection between his ideas and those of Rousseau. Rousseau's vindication of the dignity of the life of peasants, as containing in it the opportunity, and even the best opportunity, for the exercise of all the higher powers of human nature, found an instant sympathetic echo in the breast of the poet of the lakes. And there was something even in the one-sided hatred of " luxury," characteristic of Rousseau, which was not altogether repugnant to Wordsworth. Reared among a race of simple, though not untrained or ignorant, rustics of strong self-respecting character, Wordsworth cared little for any but those primary spiritual interests of human life, which seemed to him to be as fully secured in his native hills as anywhere. The doctrine that the worth of man's life is not to be measured by differences of culture any more than by differences of rank or wealth, was to him an easily learnt lesson. In fact, he tells us that in this respect the principles of the Revolution seemed to him almost axiomatic.

"If at the first great outbreak I rejoiced
  Less than might well befit my youth, the cause
  In part lay there, that unto me the events
  Seemed nothing out of nature's certain course—
  A gift that was come rather late than soon."

But in Wordsworth's mind the doctrine was deprived of the baser ingredients of fanatical bitterness and envy, which so often tainted the assertion of the essential equality of men in Rousseau and his followers. Wordsworth had too genuine a belief in the superiority of a life of simple cares and pleasures to feel any such bitterness ; he was tempted rather to pity than to envy those who diverged from his ideal of " plain living and high thinking." The levelling spirit of the Revolution, therefore, appears in him in a purified form, as a belief that " God hath chosen the weak things of the world to confound the mighty."

Yet, after all, the one-sidedness of the revolutionary spirit has not quite disappeared in Wordsworth : it shows itself in the set bent of his mind to exalt that which the world has generally despised or neglected. When he declared in one of his earliest poems that

"He who feels contempt for any living thing,
  Hath faculties which he hath never used,"

he was expressing a thought which is never far

from his mind, and which frequently shows itself in his selection of subjects. The world of polite literature was scandalised in his own day—and it can scarcely be said to have ceased yet to be scandalised—by his choice of pedlars and waggoners, peasants and beggars, for the heroes and protagonists of his verse ; but to Wordsworth such a choice was almost inevitable. As Mr. Morley says that Rousseau would not have been Rousseau, " if he had felt it shameful or derogatory " to marry a kitchen wench ; so we may fairly assert that Wordsworth would not have been Wordsworth, if he had not thought a leech-gatherer a better hero than a king. His constant tendency to assert the sanctity, the essential nobility and poetic beauty of modes of life, feelings, and interests, to which superficial associations — and sometimes even associations that are not quite superficial — of degradation and meanness are usually attached, is seen in poems like *Peter Bell*, *The Idiot Boy*, *Goody Blake and Harry Gill*, etc. Even one who is a most orthodox believer in the Wordsworthian creed, and who has tried to follow it in purging his mind of all artificial associations, may feel his faith falter at some of these performances.

Yet we need not suppose that they were the result of any conscious determination in Wordsworth to write up to a particular theory. He tells us, indeed, in one of his prefaces, that " humble and rustic life was generally chosen " for the subject of his verse, " because in that condition the essential passions of the heart find a better soil in which they can attain their maturity, are less under restraint, and speak a plainer and more emphatic language ; because in that condition of life our elementary feelings exist in a state of greater simplicity, and consequently may be more accurately contemplated and more forcibly communicated ; because the manners of rural life germinate from those elementary feelings, and from the necessary character of rural occupations are more easily comprehended and more durable; and, lastly, because in that condition the passions of men are incorporated with the beautiful and permanent forms of nature." [1] But this theory was developed *ex post facto* as the vindication of a practice which had flowed in the first instance from the natural tendencies of his mind.

We may regret the exaggeration, the human " too much," which, in cases like those above mentioned, repels many from Wordsworth, or prevents them from duly estimating his genius ; but it must be clear to every careful reader that it would be impossible to separate this element from

[1] *Poems,* vi. p. 308.

his poems without taking away at the same time that which gives them their characteristic power. A tone of sentiment which is half-democratic and half-Christian, and which will not tolerate any monopolies of good, is present in all his greater poems, and, indeed it breaks from his lips almost unconsciously at every turn. For him, poetry, wisdom, heroism, are the common property of mankind : all the deeper experiences of life are those that belong to every one ; and even " pleasure is spread through the earth in stray gifts, to be claimed by whoever shall find." [1] In his treatment of the question of education Words- worth sometimes reminds us of Rousseau's attack upon art and science, so firmly is he convinced that the " substantial things " are within the reach of every one, and that all we get by wider culture scarcely compensates for that unsettling of the natural balance of mind which culture often brings with it.

Even his æsthetic theory, to which we have already referred, that poetry is only a selection of the " language of real life," and is inferior to that language at its best, springs from the same root. He is so determined to correct the error of those

> " Who, while they most ambitiously set forth
> Extrinsic differences, the outward marks

---

[1] Cf. *Poems*, iii. 75 ; v. 373-4 ; vi. 13.

Whereby society has parted man
From man, *neglect the universal heart*,"

that he will scarcely admit the existence of any
differences which affect the spiritual life at all, if it
be not a difference *in favour* of those who lead the
simplest life.   Mr. Hutton, in his criticism upon
Wordsworth, has spoken of his " spiritual frugality " in making the most of every simple occasion,
and refraining from any waste of the sources of
emotion ; but the secret of this frugality is
Wordsworth's belief that there is little difference
between small and great occasions, and that, if we
cannot find the greatest meanings in the most
familiar experiences, we will find them nowhere.

" Long have I loved what I behold—
The night that calms, the day that cheers ;
The common growth of mother-earth
Suffices me—her tears and mirth,
Her humblest mirth and tears.
These given, what more need I desire
To stir, to soothe, to elevate,
What nobler marvels than the mind
May in life's daily prospect find,
May find, or there create ? "

3. The deepest source of this love of simple
things is that faith in man, in each man, and all
men, which was also the animating principle of
Rousseau.   Even Rousseau, however, was not a

pure individualist, but based the greatness of the individual on the fact that the *raison commune* speaks within him, and that he can be made into an organ of the *volonté générale*. And Wordsworth, who had, as was to be expected, a much deeper apprehension of this truth, tells us in the *Prelude* that he found the explanation of the immediate failure of the French Revolution in the fact that the Revolutionists forgot the unity of humanity and the continuity of its development. In the first enthusiasm of his youthful Republicanism, he had hoped to see

> " The man to come parted as by a gulf
> From him who had been."

But his disappointment taught him to

> " Trust the elevation which had made him one
> With the great family that still survives
> To illuminate the abyss of ages past,
> Sage, warrior, prophet, hero."

And to believe that there is

> " One great society alone on earth,
> The noble living and the noble dead."

And the effect of this belief in the solidarity of man, was shown in Wordsworth's intense sympathy with the *national* struggles of Spain and Germany against Napoleon. Yet, on the whole, we have to admit that this idea did not carry him very far. He apprehended it, but it did not *possess* him as he was possessed by the ideas we have already mentioned. He is not the poet of the unity and the progress of humanity ; perhaps the poet whom that idea shall inspire has yet to arise. What Wordsworth, like Rousseau, loves to speak of is rather the power and dignity of the individual man, and how he can attain to " freedom in himself " under all circumstances.

The *Prelude*, in which Wordsworth gives an account of his own spiritual development, is one of the numerous echoes of the *Confessions* of Rousseau ; but it is an echo in which the morbid and unhealthy self-analysis of the *Confessions* has all but disappeared, and in which the interest of the reader is claimed on grounds which are all but independent of the mere individual. Wordsworth seeks to exhibit to us, not so much of his own personal career, as the way in which, amid the difficulties of the time, a human soul might find peace and inward freedom. He rejects any claim to exceptional privilege, and takes his stand upon the rights of simple humanity.

> " There's not a man
> That lives, who hath not known his godlike hours
> And feels not what an empire we inherit,
> As natural beings in the strength of nature ! "

He bids us find a confirmation of our spiritual
destiny even in the childish appetite for wonder.

> "Our childhood sits,
> Our simple childhood sits upon a throne,
> That hath more power than all the elements."

And the highest effect of natural grandeur of the
glories of the Alps, for him, is that it makes us
conscious that

> "Our destiny, our being's heart and home,
> Is with infinitude, and only there;
> With hope it is, hope that can never die,
> Effort, and expectation, and desire,
> And something even more about to be!"

Lastly, out of this sense of the spiritual greatness, the "godhead" of human nature, springs
what we might call, in philosophical terms, the
optimism of Wordsworth—his assertion that good
is stronger than evil, and even that the latter is
but a means of the development of the former.
"The godhead which is ours," he says, "can never
utterly be shamed or stilled," and

> "The immortal spirit, with godlike power,
> Informs, creates, and thaws the deepest sleep
> That time can lay upon her."

Wordsworth's optimism, if it may be so called,
has no fear of sorrow or of evil. He can stand
in the shadow of death and pain, ruin and failure,

with a sympathy that is almost painful in its quiet intensity ; yet the sense " of something far more deeply interfused " which makes " our noisy years seem moments in the being of the eternal silence "; the faith in the omnipotence " of love and man's unconquerable mind," is never destroyed or even weakened in him. The contemplation of evil and pain always ends with him, by an inevitable recoil, in an inspired expression of his faith in the good which transmutes and transfigures it, as clouds are changed into manifestations of the sunlight they strive to hide. It is this spiritual recoil against the pressure of evil that draws from Wordsworth some of the loftiest and purest notes which his music ever reached, notes in which the minor tones of sorrow are made the means of expressing a deeper joy :—

> " Sighing, I turned away ; but ere
> Night fell I heard, or seemed to hear,
> Music that sorrow comes not near—
>   A ritual hymn,
> Chanted in love that casts our fear
>   By Seraphim."

THE PROBLEM OF PHILOSOPHY AT THE PRESENT TIME

PHILOSOPHY as the Effort to Reconcile the Three Terms of Thought : the World, the Self, and God—Agnosticism of Mr. Spencer and others—Combination of Subjective Idealism and Materialism—Comte's Attempt to Substitute a Subjective Synthesis for the Objective Synthesis of Philosophy—Relation of Comte's Theory to Pure Individualism—Difficulties of an Objective Synthesis —Philosophy not Creative, but a Critical Reconstruction of Belief—Exemplified in the Critical Reconstruction of Greek Belief by Plato and Aristotle—Likeness and Difference of the Modern Problem of Philosophy—Christianity as Determining the Nature of the Problem—Relation of Philosophy to Science.

In complying with the request which you have done me the honour to make, to deliver the introductory address to this Society,[1] I think that, instead of treating of any special philosophical subject, it will be more profitable to make some general remarks on the nature and objects of the study to which the Society is devoted. I propose, therefore, to say something as to the general problem of philosophy, and the special forms which that problem has taken in recent times. In doing so, it will not be possible for me to avoid an appearance of dogmatism, as I must make some assertions which are much disputed, the objections to which I shall not have time to discuss. But instead of interpolating any cheap formulas of modesty, I venture simply to make this apology once for all, and to ask you to adopt, for the time, a point of view which may not be your own. Afterwards you can avenge yourselves for this temporary submission by subjecting my words to

[1] An Introductory Address, delivered to the Philosophical Society of the University of Edinburgh, 1881.

what criticism you think fit. A philosophic temper is shown, above all things, in the power of entering into the views of another, and taking them for the moment almost as if they were your own, without prejudice to the subsequent critical reaction, which will be effective just in proportion to the degree of your previous sympathetic appreciation of the ideas criticised.

What, then, is the task of philosophy? What is its task in general, and how is that task modified by the circumstances of the present time? To the first of these questions, I answer that, stated in very general terms, the task of philosophy is to gain, or rather perhaps to regain, such a view of things as shall reconcile us to the world and to ourselves. The need for philosophy arises out of the broken harmony of a spiritual life, in which the different elements or factors seem to be set in irreconcilable opposition to each other ; in which, for example, the religious consciousness, the consciousness of the infinite, is at war with the secular consciousness, the consciousness of the finite ; or again, the consciousness of the self, with the consciousness of the external world. It is easy to see this, if we reflect on the nature of the controversies which most trouble us at present. They all, directly or indirectly, turn upon the difficulty of reconciling the three great terms of thought,—

the world, self, and God : the difficulty of carrying
out to their legitimate consequences what seem to
be our most firmly based convictions as to any one
of these factors in our intellectual life, without re-
jecting in whole or in part the claims of the others.

Thus, for example, many writers in the present
time find it impossible to admit the truth and
solidity of the principles and methods of physical
science in relation to the material world, without
extending their application beyond that world.
Yet, if we make this extension, and treat these
methods and principles as universal, we inevitably
reduce consciousness, thought, and will, to the
level of physical phenomena, and make even their
existence an insoluble problem.   Others, again,
find it difficult to assert the truth, that the consciousness of self enters into all our experience,
without reducing that experience to a series of
states of the individual soul.   And others, like
Mr. Spencer and Professor Huxley, poised between these two conflicting currents of thought,
have adopted the odd, and we might even say
irrational, expedient of telling us that we may
regard the world *either* as a collection of the
phenomena of mind, *or* as a collection of the
phenomena of matter, but that we can never bring
these two ways of looking at things together—a
view which supposes man to be afflicted with a

kind of intellectual *strabismus*, so that he can never see with one of his mental eyes without shutting the other. Again, looking beyond this conflict of materialism and subjective idealism, the intellectual unity of our life is disturbed by the opposition of the consciousness of the infinite to the consciousness of the finite. To many of our scientific men it seems axiomatic that all our real knowledge is of that which belongs to the context of a finite experience, and that all religious and metaphysical efforts to reach beyond the finite are attempts to think the unknown and unknowable. Yet such men often feel strongly the need, and, from their point of view, the extreme difficulty, of finding anything to give to the moral life of man that support which was once found in the belief that these dreams are realities. On the other hand, there are not a few men in our day,— like the hero of that remarkable little book called *Mark Rutherford*, — men whose very life is in religious ideas, yet who have imbibed from the literature of the time a conviction that such ideas must be illusory, and who therefore dwell, as it were, in a world of eclipse and paralysis, neither able to find a faith nor to do without one, sitting

" by the poisoned springs of life,
Waiting for the morrow that shall free them from the strife."

Now, it is impossible, so long as our ultimate thought of the world is thus in discord with itself, that our lives should be what human lives have sometimes been—impossible that we should rise to that energy of undivided will and affection, that free play of concentrated intelligence, that sense of the infinite resources of the spirit that moves us, out of which the highest achievements of men at all times have sprung. Nor, after the unity of our first instinctive faith has been broken by difficulties such as those I have mentioned, is it possible entirely to recover it, except by some kind of philosophical reflection. Bacon said that in the last period of ancient civilisation philosophy took the place of religion, and the same is to some extent true now. In face of the modern spirit of criticism, it is rarely possible for educated men, and for students of philosophy it is impossible, to rest for the entire support of their spiritual life upon the simple intuitions of faith. For them the age of unconsciousness is past, and they must call in the aid of reflection, if it were only to heal the wounds of reflection itself. As the builders of the second Temple had to work with arms by their side, so, in our day, those who seek either to maintain, or to replace, the old Christian synthesis of life, must provide themselves with the weapons of philosophy. It is not of our own choice that we have been born in an age of criticism ; but being here, and being by our education brought face to face with all the prevalent currents of thought, we have only two alternatives before us ; we must face our difficulties, or we must suppress them. Do we resolve to suppress them?—we see often enough what kind of moral temper comes of *that*,—the fevered fanatical spirit that founds its faith on the impossibility of knowing anything, and determines to believe, because it dare not do otherwise. Yet, if we are not content with such faith, we must seek the reconciliation of the contradictory elements of our consciousness in some new reflective synthesis, in other words, in philosophy.

The task of philosophy then, I repeat, is to rise to such a general view of things as shall reconcile us, or enable us to reconcile ourselves, to the world and to ourselves. This vague statement, however, might easily be admitted by many who will be startled and repelled when we draw out its meaning. For it means no less than this, that philosophy, by the very condition of its life, is forced to attempt what Comtists have called an " objective," or what perhaps might more properly be termed an "absolute" synthesis. It is true that many philosophers, and even great philosophers, have tried to evade this necessity, and to narrow the problem of philosophy within limits which made its solution seem easier. Especially in times of transition, when social bonds have become relaxed, and religious faith has been weakened or destroyed, philosophy also has generally lowered its claims, and has been content to abandon the great world to chaos, if only it could secure some little cosmos of its own. To these causes of diffidence in philosophy others in recent times have been added ; for our very widening knowledge of the universe has thrown a shadow of suspicion upon the attempt to measure it, and has inclined us to narrow our views to a solution of the problem of human life, and to disconnect it from the problem of the unity of all things. Can we not, it is natural to ask, find a meaning in our own lives without spelling out the secret of the universe? Can we not build our fragile houses of mortality on something less than an eternal foundation? With the growth of our knowledge grows also the consciousness of our ignorance, and more and more the latter seems to reduce the former into something merely relative and transitional. Looking out upon the wide sea of knowledge, with some measure of appreciation of its extent, it seemed but reasonable for one like Comte to say, that an " objective synthesis," a systematic view of the world as a whole, was beyond the reach of man ;

and that, if his life was to be brought into harmony with itself on a basis of knowledge, he must content himself with a "subjective synthesis," a synthesis which leaves out all speculation in relation to the greater whole of the universe, and attempts only to gather knowledge to a focus in the interests of man.

In taking up this position, Comte, it has been urged by his followers, showed a true insight into our needs as rational beings, who must desire to bring our lives into harmony and unity with themselves, and to found that harmony and unity upon an intelligent view of the facts of our condition ; and he showed at the same time a right appreciation of the limits which are set around us as finite creatures, standing in the face of a universe, the ultimate meaning of which is hidden from us by the weakness of our mental capacity and the narrowness of our opportunities.

Comte's view of things is thus based upon two incontrovertible facts — the limitation of man's powers and the imperative wants of his moral being. The old aspiring religious and philosophical synthesis, he argues, has been discredited for ever by our knowledge of the immensity of the universe and of our own feebleness. It is impossible for the creature of a day to see things *sub specie æternitatis*, for a finite mind to carry back the infinity of the universe to its central principle, to view it as a harmonious system, and, like God, to pronounce it " very good." But yet there remains the inextinguishable requirement of a rational and moral nature to rise above chance impulses and energies, and to find some one guiding principle of thought and action which shall make his life harmonious with itself. And this principle, since we cannot find it in an Absolute, whom we do *not* know, we must find in man— man individual, or man social—whom we *do* know. Renouncing, therefore, all questions as to the system of the universe, even the question whether it *is* a system, we can still draw back upon ourselves and find and produce system and harmony in our own lives. Or, if this is impossible for us as regards the fragmentary existence of the individual, we may yet detect in the history of the human race a tendency towards unity and organisation, to which all the great and good of the past have contributed, and we may give value and completeness to our individual lives by making them the instruments of this " increasing purpose."

The question which Comte thus brings home to us is, as I have already indicated, not a new one. It is the question whether it is possible to have a religion—*i.e.*, " a free convergence of all man's

affections and energies" to one object, without
a God ; and a philosophy, *i.e.*, a synthesis or
gathering to one focus of all knowledge, without
an Absolute.[1] And this is a question that has
been raised more or less distinctly in every era of
transition, when the "native hue" of human
resolution has been "sicklied o'er with a pale cast
of thought," and when men have been fain to
gather up the fragments that remained in the ship-
wreck of their greater faiths and hopes. The
individualism of the Stoics, Epicureans, and Scep-
tics, for example, corresponding as it did with the
decay of ancient religion and social morality, was
in great measure a result of such a temper of mind.
As men gave up the hope of organising their own
social relations, and of understanding the world as
an intelligible order, they fell back upon the idea
of an inner life, which might maintain harmony
with itself in the face even of an outward chaos.
Philosophy, it began to be said, is indeed, not to
penetrate into the secret of the world, which is
impenetrable, but to teach us our limits and to
make us content with them. *Tecum habita et
noris quam sit tibi curta supellex.* Yet that *curta
supellex* is enough ; the peace of inward unity
may be attained, even if we know nothing and

[1] Cf. *The Unity of Comte's Life and Doctrine*, by J. H. Bridges.
London : Trübner & Co., 1866.

can do nothing in the world without. Sure of nothing else, the individual may be sure of himself, and in the strength of a mind centred and at rest in itself, may cease to concern himself with things that can only touch the outward life.

Si fractus illabatur orbis,
Impavidum ferient ruinæ.

Now, I need not dwell on the self-contradiction of this extreme of "subjective" synthesis, in which all that is without is abandoned to chaos or uncertainty, in order that the integrity of the inner life may be preserved. It is a commonplace of philosophy that we cannot thus withdraw into ourselves and leave the world to wander its own wise or unwise way, inasmuch as the two terms thus separated by abstraction are essentially united, and our experience of the world *is* our experience of ourselves. The life of reason or consciousness is essentially a life that goes beyond itself, and in which the inward cannot be absolutely fenced off from the outward without itself ceasing to have any meaning or content. It is a life of *knowledge*, in which we can know ourselves, only as we know the universe of which, as individuals, we form a part. It is a life of *action*, in which we can realise ourselves, only by becoming the servants of an end which is being realised in the world. Concentrate

consciousness entirely upon itself, and its unreflected light will cease to shine. The world
without and the world within are not two separate
worlds, but necessary counterparts of each other ;
and, just in the extent to which we succeed in
withdrawing from the world without, we narrow
the world within.

The attitude, therefore, of the Stoic or Sceptic
who turns away from a world which he surrenders
to chaos and unreason, or in which, at least, he
gives up the hope of seeing or producing any
rational order, and who seeks thus to find all truth
and happiness within, is essentially irrational. He
is striving to realise in isolation a life whose
essential characteristic is community. He is seeking to save the life of the seed, which must be cast
into the ground and die, that it may live, by
keeping it shut up from all external influences.
For the Christian law of self-sacrifice, " he that
would save his life must lose it," is nothing more
than the transcription into terms of morality of
that which is the general law of spiritual life—a life
whose riches are always for the individual exactly
measured by the extent to which he breaks down
the limits of a self-centred individuality, to find
himself again in the larger existence of the whole.

But if this be the case, and if it is impossible
to solve the problem of the inner life without

solving the apparently wider problem of the outer life, or to base on a purely subjective synthesis a reconciliation of the spirit with itself, such as was formerly based on the objective synthesis of religion or philosophy, equally impossible is it to draw any other absolute line of division, such, for example, as that between the life of the nation and the life of humanity, or again, between the life of humanity and the course of nature.   In every similar division we are separating elements so correlated that the meaning of each one of them begins to evaporate so soon as we realise what we have done in separating it from the rest.   To make such an abstraction must introduce a fatal discord between the practical life of man, and the facts upon which we pretend to base it.   And indeed, as I think can be shown in the case of Comte, such an attempt involves the self-deception of treating that as absolute and divine, which we at the same time admit to be uncertain and transitory.[1]   How, for example, can we make a God out of humanity, if we think of mankind as a race of beings which is not really organic, but in which there is only a general tendency to organisation, a tendency, which again is subjected to an immeasurable external contingency?   Comte's

[1] I have attempted to show this in my book on *The Social Philosophy and Religion of Comte.*

attempt to escape the great difficulties which con-
fessedly beset an optimistic creed—the creed that
in some way all things work together for good—
by thus falling back from the assertion of system
in the universe, to the assertion of system only
in the life of man, like most compromises, unites
all the difficulties of both extremes it would avoid ;
the difficulties of an absolute philosophy, which
seems to go beyond the limits of human knowledge, and the difficulties of a scepticism, which
leaves the moral and intellectual life of man without a principle of unity. The Stoic or Sceptic
who bids us concentrate ourselves on our own
soul, and the Positivist, who bids us worship
humanity, are equally bidding us treat a part,
which we can know and understand only as a part,
as if it were the whole. They are attempting
to break in one place only the indivisible unity
of the intelligence and the intelligible world ;
but if that unity be broken in one place it is
wholly destroyed. *Falsus in uno, falsus in omni-*
bus. For it is a unity which is not like a particular
hypothesis, that may be asserted or denied without
detriment to the rest of our knowledge, but it is
the hypothesis, if we may so call it, which is
implied in all knowledge whatever, the hypothesis
which constitutes our rational being. Hence Kant
showed a true sense of the conditions of philo-

sophical synthesis, when he said that, if it could be shown that there was one metaphysical problem with which his *Critique of Pure Reason* was incompetent to deal, it must be regarded as an entire failure. If philosophy is incapable of a universal synthesis, it cannot make any synthesis at all. If it admit any absolute division, whether between the ego and the non-ego, or between man and nature, or even between the finite and infinite, it is driven of necessity into scepticism. Unless it reconciles us with the universe, it cannot even reconcile us with ourselves. The present is a time in which there are many voices to welcome the well-known saying of Pope:

> " Know well thyself, presume not God to scan,
>   The proper study of mankind is man ";

but the simple, yet demonstrable answer to such partial Agnosticism is, that if we cannot, in the sense I have indicated, know God, we cannot know anything.

But if this be so, if we cannot give up the idea of a universal synthesis, without practically giving up philosophy altogether, we must not hide from ourselves the enormous difficulties with which philosophy has to contend, difficulties which seem to grow every day with our increasing knowledge of man and of the world in which he lives. For all this knowledge seems to be making wider and wider the division between the individual and the universal, between the vision of short-sighted, changeable creatures such as men seem to be, and the all-embracing whole. These difficulties, however, though they by no means disappear, yet somewhat change their character when we consider that the work of philosophy is not in the first instance constructive, but rather critical and reconstructive ; that its business is not to seek for something transcendent, some hypothesis as to things hitherto unknown and alien to our experience, but rather to bring to light the hypothesis, if we choose to call it so, on which our rational being is founded. Philosophy must necessarily seem to be something extravagant and wildly ambitious to any one who does not discern that the problem it would solve is not one which arbitrarily, or as a matter merely of curiosity, we *choose* to solve, but one which we have in some way been solving, or of which we have been presupposing the solution, at every moment of our lives. To rise from the finite to the infinite would be impossible, if the consciousness of the infinite were not already involved in the consciousness of the finite, and developed along with it. Philosophy is not a first venture into a new field of thought, but the re-thinking of a secular and religious consciousness, which has been developed, in the main, independently of philosophy. It was the great work of Kant to show that experience itself is possible only through the necessity and universality of thought. But in thus proving the relativity of the finite objects of experience to the intelligence (which is not itself such an object), he really showed,—though without himself being fully conscious of it, and almost, we might say, against his will,—that we cannot admit the validity of the empirical consciousness without admitting the validity of the consciousness of that which, in the narrower sense of the word, is beyond experience.

Hence, to one who follows out the Kantian principles to their legitimate result, it becomes impossible to treat the objective synthesis of religion as the illusion of a finite mind trying to stretch itself beyond its proper limits. The religious takes its place beside the secular consciousness, the consciousness of the infinite beside the consciousness of the finite world, as the consciousness of a real object, or rather of the ultimate reality upon which everything else rests. And philosophy, in dealing with the one as with the other, is discharged from the absurd and impossible feat of finding its way into a transcendent region beyond all consciousness and experience. In both cases, in relation to the infinite as in relation to the finite world, the work of philosophy goes beyond the primary unreflected consciousness of man only in this aspect, that it brings that consciousness to a deeper understanding of itself. In both we have a right to begin our task of criticism and reconstruction with a faith in the great work achieved in and by the spirit of man in the past ; and we ought to begin it with the consciousness that *our* criticism and reconstruction can have value only as a continuation of that work. For it is this consciousness that alone can justifiably raise us above the feeling of our own weakness for the task which is laid upon philosophy in our time, and can save us from the intruding suspicion, that in his religions and his philosophies man has been perpetually renewing the history of Babel—attempting to build a tower that shall reach to heaven, only to find the work again and again stopped by the confusion of languages among the builders. If, therefore, philosophy may be described as a critical reconstruction of belief, we must recollect that this reconstruction, from a higher point of view, is merely development ; or, to put it more simply, we must remember that, in philosophy as in other things, the hope of mankind for the future must be a vain illusion, unless it can reasonably be based on a deep reverence for the past.

In the " Faust " of Goethe, the poet who of all others has most deeply fathomed and expressed the conflict of the modern spirit with itself— though it may perhaps be said that, like a physician strong in diagnosis but not in therapeutics, he often stops at the description of disease, and finds his own poetic deliverance from it simply in thus describing it [1]—we find some words that may be applied to the work of philosophy.   When Faust utters all his despair of life in that comprehensive curse in which he disowns every faith, and even every illusion that has hitherto supported mankind, the chorus of spirits breaks in with a song, in which lament over what has been lost is mingled with a far-off hint of the only possible restoration—

> " Woe, woe, thou hast destroyed it,
> The beautiful world,
> With mighty blow ;
> It trembles, it falls to ruins.
> A Demigod hath broken it down.
> We bear away the ruins into nothingness,
> And lament over the lost beauty."

---

[1] " Physician of the iron age,
Goethe has done his pilgrimage.
He took the suffering human race,
He read each wound, each weakness clear,
And struck his finger on the place,
And said : ' *Thou ailest here, and here !* ' "
         Arnold's Poems, Memorial Verses, April, 1850.

And then the song goes on—

> " Mighty One
>   Of the sons of earth,
>   With greater majesty
>   Build it up,
>   In thine own soul build it up again ;
>   A new course of life
>   Begin,
>   With fresh unclouded sense,
>   And let new songs rise
>   In place of those that are silenced."

" In thine own soul build it up again,"—this is the ever-repeated call to philosophy at all times, such as the present, when the first unity of faith and reason is disturbed. But the task has become, if in some respects a harder, yet in other respects a more hopeful one in modern times. That this is so may be shown by a short comparison of the form in which the problem presented itself to Plato and Aristotle, with the form in which it presents itself to us. In Plato's *Republic*, we find an attempt to " build up again in the soul " of the philosopher the falling edifice of Greek civilisation, to restore its religious and political life, by going back to the ideal principle on which it rested. But the difficulty of such restoration lay in this, that the first intuitive synthesis of Greece was a synthesis of the imagination, in which that which was essentially limited and national was treated as unlimited and universal. Greek morality did not look beyond the boundary of the nation, seldom even beyond the boundary of the civic state. Greek religion, as it was an apotheosis of the special gifts of the Greek genius, was in some measure a consecration of the national spirit of exclusion. Hence, neither religion nor morality could offer an effective resistance to the disintegrating power of reflection. As it was mainly the poetic imagination which had peopled Olympus with the fair humanities of the gods, the power of Greek religion disappeared almost as soon as the people became capable of distinguishing poetry from prose. And as, in the ethical life of the Greek state, the local and temporal was rather confused than reconciled with that which is universal, it fell an easy prey to the casuistry of the Sophists. On the other hand the scepticism of the Sophists remained superficial and rhetorical, just because it found so little power of resistance in the institutions which it attacked. When, therefore, philosophy in Plato and Aristotle set itself to the task of reconstructing the synthesis upon which the moral and intellectual life of Greece was founded, and restoring the broken harmony of faith and reason, its reconciliation was necessarily imperfect, because of the imperfection of the positive and negative elements which it sought to reconcile. It tried to combine the freedom of thought, which had shown itself in the Sophistic movement, with the substantial contents of Greek life, morality, and religion, which Sophistry had rejected. But the freedom and universality of thought was in essential conflict with the limited character of the contents ; and even to Plato himself a merely imaginative religion could not be more than a " noble lie," *i.e.*, a truth veiled under an inadequate sensuous form. The element of philosophy in which the reconciliation was attempted, was itself fatal to the reconciliation aimed at. Hence already in Plato we find the beginning of that withdrawal into the inner life from an unideal world, which was carried out in subsequent philosophy, and which of necessity ended in the self-contradiction of scepticism.

The modern movement from faith to reason bears a striking analogy to the movement of ancient thought. Yet there are important differences, which make the struggle of tendencies in modern times harder and more obstinate, but which also for that very reason enable us to anticipate a more satisfactory result. Here, too, we have a system of religion apprehended by the intuitive consciousness of faith, and manifesting itself in definite forms of intellectual and social life. Here, too, we have the spirit of reflection after a time awakening and subjecting the whole religious system, as well as all the institutions founded upon it, to a searching, and often a destructive criticism. And here, too, we find philosophy attempting to restore the broken harmony of man's consciousness of himself and of the world, by separating the permanent from the transitory elements of his earlier faith. But, beneath this general similarity of development there are many points of contrast : which we may roughly sum up by saying that the first synthesis of Christendom took the form of a religion which was not national but universal, and that the negative movement against it has been not merely analytic and sophistic, but also scientific, and, therefore, within certain limits, constructive. Hence, also, just because of the deeper spiritual meaning and fuller development of the two seemingly opposed powers that divide our life, we have some reason to think that it may be possible to combine what is good in both, and to attain to a philosophical synthesis, which may be not merely provisional but of permanent value for mankind. Let me say a few more words on each of these points.

The religion of Greece was, as I have said, national, not universal, and for that very reason it was essentially a religion of the artistic imagination ; for it is the imagination which lifts the part into a whole, and makes a particular into a substitute for the universal. It has been called an anthropomorphic religion ; but, as Hegel has remarked, in the higher sense it was not anthropomorphic enough,—it lifted some human qualities into the divine, but not humanity itself as such. Its gods were ideal figures, humanised rather than human, fixed like statues in the eternal repose of beauty, and lifted above all the narrowing conditions of human life. Christianity, on the other hand, brought down the divine into the form of an individual life lived under those conditions, struggling with the wants and pains of mortality and the opposition of fellow mortals, and undergoing and accepting the common lot of renunciation, sorrow, and death. It thus idealised, not choice specimens of intelligence and valour, but humanity itself, in its simplest and humblest form of life. It taught the world not to regard the ideal as something which a few elect spirits might reach, by escaping from the commonplace of existence, but to find it in the commonplace itself ; to make the limits of mortality the means of freedom, and to turn pain, death, and even evil into forms of the manifestation of good. Now this optimism on the very basis of pessimism, whose Christ has "descended into hell," this idealisation of ordinary reality as it stands without selection or change, just because it was *this*, was no religion of phantasy, of art, of the poetic imagination merely. It did not flinch from the facts of life, however dark and threatening, or seek to turn its eyes to some earthly paradise lifted above the clouds and the winds. Art in it was secondary, not primary ; in its poetry truth was bursting through the sensuous veil. And from this it necessarily follows that it is not a dream that vanishes with a waking of the prosaic consciousness in either of its shapes, either as the distinct commonsense apprehension of fact, or as the reflective analysis of thought. Whatever changes of form, therefore, it has been, and may yet be subjected to (and I do not say that these will be small), the Christian view of the world in its essence is based upon such a simple acknowledgment of the truth and reality of things, that it need not fear overthrow, even from our widening knowledge of the facts of life, or from the deeper self-consciousness to which reflection is gradually bringing us. In the midst even of apparent rejection, its ideals have maintained and increased their hold over the emancipated intelligence of Europe, and its fundamental conception of life penetrates and moulds the social and religious speculations of those who, like Comte, seem to have most thoroughly renounced it.

On the other hand, if the first intuitional basis of modern life is thus strong in itself, strong too, it must be acknowledged, are the powers that assail it. The sophistic culture that undermined the old beliefs of Greece, and the morality founded upon them, was but a feeble solvent, compared with the disintegrating force of negative reflection and scientific criticism, to which *our* faiths are subjected. The boldness of the ancient sceptic was chilled by a sense of the weakness of his own position. He might set the human against the divine, the individual against the State, the finite and relative against the infinite and absolute ; but he was paralysed by the negative character of his own teaching, by the consciousness that his emancipation of the intellect was a process whereby it was emptied of all contents, and that his liberation of the individual from limited social bonds could lead to nothing better than anarchy. In modern times, on the other hand, it has ceased to be so. The world of finite interests and objects has rounded itself, as it were, into a separate whole, within which the mind of man can fortify itself, and live *securus adversus deos*, in independence of the infinite. In the sphere of *thought*, there has been forming itself an ever-increasing body of science, which, tracing out the relation of finite things to finite things, never finds it necessary to seek for a beginning or an end to its infinite series of phenomena, and which meets the claims of theology with the saying of the astronomer, " I do not need that hypothesis." In the sphere of *action*, again, the complexity of modern life presents a thousand isolated interests, crossing each other in ways too subtle to trace out—interests commercial, social, and political— in pursuing one or other of which the individual may find ample occupation for his existence, without ever feeling the need of any return upon himself, or seeing any reason to ask himself whether this endless striving has any meaning or object beyond itself. Nor need we wonder that the prevailing school of philosophy is one that renounces all such questions as vain, and bids us be content to know that we can know nothing. The very wealth of modern life and science, both because it makes the ultimate synthesis more difficult, and because it supplies us with such a fulness of interests independent of that synthesis, tends to drive us back to the old simple Agnostic philosophy of the Persian poet, Omar Khayyam :—

" Myself when young did eagerly frequent
Doctor and sage, and heard great argument

About it and about, but evermore
Came out by the same door that in I went.

" With them the seed of wisdom did I sow,
And with mine own hand wrought to make it grow ;
And this was all the harvest that I reaped ;
I came like water, and like wind I go.

" There was a door to which I found no key,
There was a veil through which I could not see.
Some little talk awhile of Me and Thee
There was : and then no more of Thee and Me."

The Agnosticism and Secularism of these latter
days, however, has a far deeper meaning than that
which we can attribute to the verses of Omar
Khayyam, or to any similar phase of opinion in
past time. It is like in expression,—as, indeed,
in the first aspect of them, all negations seem to
be much alike. But, just as the ordinary commonplaces about the sorrows and trials of life have a
greater significance when they fall from the lips
of age and experience, than when they are merely
the utterance of the first dawning thoughtfulness
of youth ; so our modern Agnosticism implies a
deeper consciousness of the problem of human
existence than could possibly have been attained
by Omar Khayyam. For it is based, not on a
mere Epicurean concentration upon the individual
life, nor on the materialism of passion, but on our
knowledge of the greatness of the universe, and

on the complexity of finite interests, both practical and scientific, which seem to stand on their own merits, and to need no reference to anything higher, in order to recommend them as sufficient objects of our lives.

A consideration of these two main elements of modern thought enables us to understand why the struggle of positive and negative tendencies —of the consciousness of the infinite with the consciousness of the finite, of the religious with the secular spirit—should be so much more violent and protracted than the analogous conflict in earlier times. A religion which is universal and not merely imaginative, and a reflection which is scientific, and not merely analytic or destructive, are each of them charged with interests vital to man ; and, so long as they are opposed as enemies, they are necessarily involved in a contest which is incapable of being decided by any final victory on one side or the other. Man, as he has an understanding, cannot but acknowledge the facts of his finite life, and in view of them he must sooner or later withdraw his allegiance from every ideal that does not prove itself to be real, and renounce every belief which is found inconsistent with the laws of thought or the nature of experience. Yet, on the other hand, as he is a self-conscious being, who knows the world in relation to the self, and who therefore cannot but realise more or less distinctly the unity of all things with each other and with the mind that knows them, he must equally reject any attempt to confine him to the finite world. Nor, however he may seek, in accordance with imperfect theories of knowledge, to limit himself to that world, can he ever really succeed in confining his thoughts within it. All our knowledge of the things of time is, so to speak, on the background of eternity itself. The scientific impulse itself presupposes the presence in our own minds of an idea of truth as the ultimate unity of being and knowing, which in all our inquiries into the laws of the universe we can only develop and verify. For it is just because we are obscurely conscious, even from the beginning, of this unity that we regard every apparent discord of things with each other as a mystery and a problem, and so are continually seeking law and unity—in other words, seeking *thought*, in things, with the confidence that ultimately it must be found there.

In like manner the practical impulse, whenever it goes beyond, as in every conscious being it must somewhat go beyond, a craving for the satisfaction of immediate sensuous wants, implies the presence in our minds of an idea of absolute good, which is at once the realisation of the self and of a divine purpose in the world. What, indeed, could we possibly hope from our feeble efforts after a good, which is only gradually defining itself before us as we advance, if we did not believe that they unite themselves with the great stream of tendency which is independent of us? How could we think to attain our " being's end and aim," if we did not regard it ultimately identical with the " divine event to which the whole creation moves " ? Hence a sober philosophy, admitting to the full all that can be said by the Agnostic about the feebleness of the powers of men as individuals, and the greatness of the universe, can yet reject the Agnostic conclusion from these premises, and can maintain that an absolute or objective synthesis is no mere dream of the childhood of the human race, when the distinction between the possible and the impossible had not yet been made, but rather that it is a task which is forced upon us by our rational nature, and which, as rational beings, we cannot but attempt to fulfil.

All thought and action, all moral and intellectual life, presupposes in us the power of looking at things, not from the point of view of our own individuality, but *in ordine ad universum* ; and whatever presumption there is in the idea of a universal synthesis is already involved in our existence as rational or self-conscious beings.

Philosophy may therefore begin its work by a vindication of the religious consciousness—the consciousness of the infinite,—as presupposed in that very consciousness of the finite, which at present often claims to exclude it altogether, or to reduce it to an empty apotheosis of the unknown and unknowable. And having thus taught us to regard the consciousness of the infinite as no mere illusion, but as the consciousness of a real object, an Absolute, a God, who has been revealing himself in and to man in all ages, philosophy must go on to consider the history of religion, and indeed the whole history of man as founded on religion, as the progressive development of this consciousness. Nor can it fail to discover that the idea on which the higher life of man is founded, —the idea of the unity of man as spiritual with an absolute Spirit,—has in Christianity been brought to light and made, in a manner, apprehensible by all. Whatever, therefore, may be the change of form to which this idea may have to submit in being applied to our ever-widening knowledge of nature and man, and whatever developments of it may be necessary ere it can solve the difficulties suggested by this increasing knowledge, we have good reason to be confident that we have in it a principle of universal synthesis which is adequate to the task.

On the other side, while this is true, it is also true that philosophy cannot conclusively meet the attacks of scientific criticism, except by coming into closer relation with the work of finite science than it has ever hitherto done ; for the only true answer to such attacks is to show that the facts and laws, upon which they rest, are capable of a higher interpretation than that which has been drawn from them by those who have attended to these facts and laws alone.   Philosophy, therefore, in face of the increasing complexity of modern life, has a harder task laid upon it than ever was laid upon it before.   It must emerge from the region of abstract principles and show itself able to deal with the manifold results of empirical science, giving to each of them its proper place and value.   If it ever could sit "upon a hill remote" to reason of "fate, free-will, foreknowledge absolute," it may not do so now.   Within, as without, the special province of philosophy, the times are past when, to give spiritual help to men, it was sufficient to have a deep intuitive apprehension of a few great principles of spiritual life, and to denounce the representatives of empirical knowledge and finite interests, as sophists, "apostles of the dismal science," and "apes of the Dead Sea."   We may be thankful to our Carlyles and Ruskins, as we are thankful in higher measure to the great men of their type in an earlier time,—men who utter in powerful language the primary truths of morality and religion,—even when they express these truths in a one-sided and intolerant way, refusing to pay due regard to the achievements of finite science, and treating with contempt every improvement that does not involve a fundamental change of man's moral being. But it is, after all, a mark of weakness to address the modern world with the unguarded utterances of an ancient prophet. To repeat against men like Mill and Darwin the old watchwords with which Plato attacked the Sophists is, to say the least of it, an anachronism ; for it is to refuse to recognise how far such men are from being Sophists, and how much of the spirit of Plato they have imbibed. And it is to forget on the other hand that philosophy has a different task from that which it had in the days of Plato, that it has abandoned the Greek dualism of form and matter, and thereby accepted the task of idealising interests and objects from which Plato might have been excused for turning away. He who would further the philosophical work of the future must renounce once for all this questionable luxury of contempt, which in this, as indeed in almost all cases, is the mortal enemy of insight. For the speculative labour of the future is one that requires the patient consideration of every partial truth, and the persistent effort to give it its due place in the whole, as well as a firm apprehension of the principles that underlie all truth. And the practical labour of the future is, not merely by a shock to awaken men to the reality of spiritual things, but to follow out the spiritual principle in its application to all the details of our physical, economical, and social condition, till we have seen how the life of each human being, and every part of that life, may be made worth living for itself. Plato speaks of an " old quarrel between the poet and the philosopher," which is to be reconciled only if poetry can be shown to be truth, or truth, in its highest aspect, to be poetry. In like manner we may say of this almost equally " old quarrel " between the prophet and the man of science, that it can be healed only by carrying back our scattered knowledge of the facts and laws of nature to the principle upon which they rest, and, on the other hand, by developing that principle so as to fill all the details of knowledge with a significance which they cannot have in themselves, but only as seen *sub specie æternitatis.*

THE GENIUS OF CARLYLE

Sources of his Influence over his Contemporaries—Its Temporary Eclipse—Merits of his Historical Works—Swift's Suggestion of a Philosophy of Clothes—Idealistic Interpretation given to it by Carlyle—His Rejection of Philosophy, and his Belief in Imaginative Intuition—"Natural Supernaturalism"—Religious Symbols as the Objects of Practical Faith—The Gospel of Work—The Age of Faith and the Age of Reflection—The Scepticism and Materialism of the Eighteenth Century—Revival of a Spiritual View of Nature and History—Carlyle's Ideal View of History and his Attitude towards Poetry—Practical Application of his Doctrines to Politics—Hero Worship—Opposition to Democracy—Defective View of Social Forces—General Lesson of his Works.

THE best way of dealing with a great author is, in the first instance, to go to him without much criticism, and with a receptive mind, and to let his way of thinking permeate into our minds, until it becomes part of their very substance. For, till we have done so, our criticism will not be adequate ; it will be wanting in sympathy, and it will rather tend to defend us against his spirit than enable us to appreciate it. When, however, we have for a long time submitted to such a powerful influence, when we have learned to live in the atmosphere of our author's ideas, so that we can almost anticipate the turn his thoughts will take on any occasion, it is advisable for us to change our method, to put him, so to speak, at arm's length, and to attempt calmly to estimate what we have got from him, and so to determine his proper place among the inhabitants of our private Walhalla—among the company of the wise to whom we return ever again and again, as the permanent possessions of our intellectual life.

A lecture delivered to the Dialectic Society of the University of Glasgow.

Such reflections as these naturally occurred to me in trying to put together a few thoughts about an author who was the greatest literary influence of my own student days.   Every new generation has a language of its own, and is spoken to, if not with the most permanent power, at least with the greatest immediate awakening effect, by the writers who are fighting their way to recognition rather than by those who have already achieved the position of classics and authorities.   And undoubtedly, at that time, Carlyle was the author who exercised the most powerful charm upon young men who were beginning to think.   It is hardly possible for those who now for the first time take up Carlyle's works to realise how potent that charm was.   " Since then many things have happened."   It would scarcely be too much to say that then this country was still outside of the main stream of European culture.   It would certainly not be too much to say that its intellectual horizon was then closed in by many limits which now, partly by Carlyle's own agency, have ceased to exist.   To name only a few points, Carlyle was the first in this country who discovered the full significance of the great revival of German literature, and the enormous reinforcement which its poetic and philosophic idealism had brought to the failing faith of man.   He was at least the first

who, in a definite and effective way, in broad and
powerfully drawn outlines, represented to us the
new ideas about man and his world which that
literature contains. He spoke, therefore, from
what was recognisably a higher point of view than
that of the ordinary sects and parties which divided
opinion in this country, a higher point of view
than any of the prevailing orthodoxies and hetero-
doxies. He spoke, besides, not only for himself,
but as representing the weight of a new learning
and culture of which we were ignorant ; and, in
addition to his own great genius, he had the
advantage of being thus the first from whom we
heard the great words of Goethe and Fichte, of
Schiller and Richter and Novalis. Nor was he
content to speak of the significance of German
thought from an abstract point of view ; he was
continually trying to show what it meant *for us*.
By the aid of the clue it put into his hands he
gave us a new interpretation of history, and
especially of those two great revolutions—the
English and the French Revolution—from which
the political, social, and religious history of this
country and of modern Europe take their new
beginning. He broke through the narrow limits
of the conventional dignity of history, not only
by an imaginative presentment of the facts which
made them spring into life again, as if they were

taking place before our eyes, but by what was almost a new kind of insight into those inner forces of belief and passion which are called into action whenever men are freed from the yoke of habit by the shock of revolution. His prophetic tones, his humour and pathos, his denunciations of cant and formalism, even the strange tricks he played with the English language, seemed to make literature a living thing, and to realise the conception of his first great book—to strip from humanity all that the tailor has done for it, and to let us see the bare sinews and muscles of the Hercules, the passions that are hidden by the conventionalities of society, the eternal faiths and hopes, without some form of which it is impossible for men to live and die. Nor was he merely a student who cast new light on the past ; he was inspired with a passion for social reform, which, at least in this country, was then felt by few. He expressed, almost for the first time in English, that disgust at the mean achievements of what we call civilisation, that generous wrath at the arbitrary limitation of its advantages, that deep craving for a better order of social life, which is the source of so many of the most important social and political movements of the present day. He set before us as our aim, not any single measure of reform, but a new idea of political and social

life, in the light of which the policy of our states-
men of both parties seemed mean and paltry. Yet
this new ideal, when we came to look at it closely,
was, after all, nothing new or strange. It was in
new words, words suited to the new time, the
expression of those religious and moral principles
which all in this country—and especially we Scots-
men—had received into ourselves almost with our
mother's milk. It was Puritanism idealised, made
cosmopolitan, freed from the narrowness which
clung to its first expression, or with which time
had encrusted it. As Goethe, in the strange tale
which Carlyle has translated, pictured the transfor-
mation of the fisherman's hut into the altar of a
new Temple of Civilisation, so Carlyle seemed to
change the old banner of the Covenant into a
standard for the forward march of mankind toward
a better ideal of human life. Thus at once widening our horizon and enkindling our enthusiasm,
speaking to us in the name of a wider culture,
and at the same time reviving the freshness of
our earliest faith, and reuniting for us the light
and the heat which were becoming divided in our
inner life—what wonder that Carlyle was listened
to with passionate admiration and reverence, such
as is felt by the young only for a great teacher
who meets and answers the questions which they
are led by the spirit of the time to ask?

Since that date, many things have changed. The great literature which Carlyle first interpreted has become known, either directly or by other channels. The narrow ways of thinking on religious and social philosophy, the narrow canons of literary criticism, against which he protested so vehemently, have lost their authority, partly through the teaching of Carlyle himself. This country has been opened up to cosmopolitan influences, and has been drawn into the main current of the great European movement of life and thought which began with the French Revolution. New forms in poetry, new methods in science, new ideas in history and philosophy, have to a great extent overpowered that insular spirit which characterised the nation during the first half of the century. Many thoughts which then seemed to be paradoxical to older men, and which young men accepted from Carlyle with a keen sense of their own intellectual audacity, have become almost commonplaces, so that the new generation is inclined rather to wonder that Carlyle should insist upon them so earnestly and so frequently. What, perhaps, tends still more to weaken his influence, —many controversies in which he took part, and which he was disposed to decide by a direct "yes" or "no," have now passed into another stage, and are seen to be incapable of settlement by so simple a method.   We must add that Carlyle, during his later years, did not become more accessible, but, according to a law to which there are few exceptions, less accessible, to new ideas.   It is an old Greek proverb that those whom the Gods love die young ; and it is at least no fortunate circumstance for an author's fame that he should survive the best expression of his thought.   In Carlyle's latest works, especially in the *Latter Day Pamphlets*, he repeated his old formulas with an increase of vehemence, but with a decrease of real force, and certainly with less perception of any limiting considerations.   And his last fourteen years of activity were spent on the somewhat uncongenial task of painting one, who, at the highest estimate of him, was the most prosaic and irreligious of modern heroes ; and the character of the work Carlyle had thus undertaken to do, tempted him to give a wilful emphasis to those one-sided dicta, which in his earlier writings seemed only the humorous exaggerations of an unpopular aspect of truth.   Finally, after a considerable interval of the silence of old age, came the indiscretions of a biographer who thought it his duty to let " the many-headed beast know " everything, even the most private details of the life of one of the most whimsical and dyspeptic of men,—a biographer, I may add, who misjudged his hero, as a man without humour was sure to misjudge one who was full of it, by taking all his extravagant statements *au pied de la lettre*.

Perhaps too much has been made of the indiscretion of a writer, who, so far as indiscreet publication was concerned, seems not to have gone much beyond what he was commissioned or allowed to do by Carlyle himself. But it is worth while to remark that there are many details of a man's life, which gain an undue importance by being revived after the lapse of years, and when it is no longer possible to supply the necessary explanation of the words and actions that express only the feelings of the passing hour. There is, it must be always remembered, a good deal even in the lives of the greatest of men that is not worth remembering (unless, indeed, we could remember everything); much which it disturbs the true light and shade, the true proportion of character, to remember. The little jealousies from which even the most generous are not free; the slight collisions of temper between those who are fundamentally in harmony; the tittle-tattle, sometimes with a shade of half-meant malice, which helps to pass the moments of relaxation—these things are but the

"   .   .   .   .   dust,
Of the windy ways of men,

That lightly rises up,
And is lightly laid again."

They have a meaning for the day, but they are essentially exaggerated if they are stored up, like flies in amber, beyond the day. The ordinary gossip of biography is interesting enough, but I must profess for myself an entire disbelief that any important additional light is thrown by it upon the character of men who have otherwise expressed themselves so fully as Carlyle. The truth of the details of such gossip is almost always incapable of being verified or set exactly in the proper light by the most careful research ; and even if you could get at it, it is seldom worth the trouble. Upon the whole, I think we shall do well to take our idea of men like Carlyle from the works in which they have revealed themselves at their best, and to refuse to be moved by the imperfect records of private life, in which, as it is impossible to state or explain everything, what is stated is generally capable of various interpretations. Especially in the case of Carlyle, I think our view will be not only more charitable, but more just, if we let him speak for himself, and if we attend most to the speech of his better days, before his eye was dimmed and his natural force abated by old age and sorrow.

The things of which I have just spoken explain

how the present generation must necessarily stand in a very different attitude to Carlyle from that in which we stood some thirty years ago. In the interval he has lost almost all the adventitious advantages which he then had, and he now speaks with certain adventitious *dis*advantages to a generation which is irritated by the near, yet unsympathetic, view of a somewhat tyrannical personality. He is seen now without any special prestige or prophetic halo round his head, as a great man indeed, yet one who no longer stands forth among smaller men of his own generation, but rather as one who has withdrawn to his place among his equals on Parnassus. It is too soon finally to settle his rank as a man of letters, a historian, and a moral teacher, apart from all exaggerating or depressing influences ; but it is not too soon to make some attempt to measure the value of his teaching, and in some approximate way to estimate the works he has left behind, both by a literary and by a moral standard—two standards which, in his case at least, cannot well be separated.

In this lecture I must content myself with indicating one or two points which must be taken into account in such an estimate, and in doing so I shall confine myself to Carlyle's directly didactic works, passing over his great historical books on the French Revolution, on Cromwell, and on

Frederic the Great with a single remark. The merits of these histories are obvious. Carlyle seldom attempts to generalise or to convey in abstract terms the meaning and spirit of a period of history, and, when he does so, his success is by no means of the highest. What he generally attempts, and achieves with supreme success, is imaginatively to realise the events and characters with which he has to deal, and to present them to us in such startling life-like colours that we almost seem to see the place and know in person the men of the story. Nor does he achieve this result by any of the deceptive scene-painting tricks of ordinary picturesque writing, but by a kind of dramatic reproduction, based on the most careful and accurate study of facts, which lets us see the inmost spirit of the *dramatis personæ* through, and along with, the outward fashion of their lives. It is scarcely too much to say that he has done for Mirabeau and Danton, Cromwell and Frederic, Voltaire and Diderot, that which Shakspere did for his characters ; he has made them visible in the clear hues of life, and at the same time transparent, so that we not only see them, but see into them. The same gift of penetrative imagination has enabled him, in the first and greatest of his historical works, not only to bring before us the outward events of the French Revolution, but almost to make us live in the streets of Paris, and feel again the wild throb of joy and terror, the fluctuation of suspicion and despair and infinite hope, first felt by those who were swept along in that great outburst of the subterranean forces of human nature. Such imaginative power of making the dead past alive again may not be all that is required of the ideal modern historian, but without it the work of the Dryasdust, the careful collector of facts, will lead to little, and the highest work of the philosophic searcher for laws and principles will be impossible.

I turn now to the more directly didactic works of Carlyle, especially to the *Sartor Resartus* (which is the authentic exposition of his view of life in its most general principles), and to the pamphlets on *Chartism*, *Past and Present*, and *The Latter Day Pamphlets*, in which he tries to apply these principles to the political and social questions of his own time.

The *Sartor Resartus* is based upon an idea which we find already in Swift, an author with whom Carlyle has many points of kindred. In the " Tale of a Tub " we read as follows :—

"About this time it happened a sect arose, whose tenets obtained and spread very far, especially in the *grand monde* and among everybody of good fashion. They worshipped a sort of idol, who, as their doctrine delivered, did daily create men by a kind of manufactory operation. This idol they placed in the highest part of the house, on an altar erected about three feet ; he was shown in the posture of a Persian Emperor, sitting on a super-ficies, with his legs interwoven under him. This god had a goose for an ensign, whence it is that some learned men pretend to deduce his original from Jupiter Capitolinus. . . .

" The worshippers of this deity had also a system of their belief which seemed to turn upon the following fundamentals. They held the uni-verse to be a large suit of clothes, which invests everything ; that the earth is invested by the air ; the air is invested by the stars ; and the stars are invested by the *primum mobile*. Look on this globe of earth, you will find it to be a very com-plete and fashionable dress. What is that which some call land but a fine coat faced with green? or the sea but a waistcoat of water-tabby? Proceed to the particular works of the creation, you will find how curious journeyman Nature has been to trim up the vegetable beaux ; observe how sparkish a periwig adorns the head of a beech, and what a fine doublet of white satin is worn by the birch. To conclude from all, what is man himself but a micro-coat, or rather a complete suit of clothes with all its trimmings? As to his body, there can be no dispute ; but examine even the acquirements of his mind.   You will find these all contribute in their order to furnishing out an exact dress.   To instance no more, is not Religion a cloak, Self-love a surtout, Vanity a shirt, and Honesty a pair of shoes, worn out in the dirt ?"

" These postulates being admitted, it will follow in due course of reasoning that those beings, which the world calls improperly suits of clothes, are in reality the most refined species of animals ; or to proceed higher, that they are rational creatures or men.   For is it not manifest that they live, and move, and talk, and perform all other offices of human life?   Are not beauty, and wit, and mien, and breeding their inseparable proprieties?   In short, we see nothing but these suits of clothes, hear nothing but them.   Is it not they who walk the streets, fill up Parliament, coffee, play-houses? It is true, indeed, that these animals which are vulgarly called suits of clothes, or dresses, do, according to certain compositions, receive different appellations.   If one of them be trimmed up with a gold chain, and a red gown, and a white rod, it is called a *Lord Mayor* ; if certain ermine and furs be placed in a certain position, we style them a *judge* ; and so, an apt conjunction of lawn and black satin, we entitle a *bishop*."

This conception or metaphor, which is at the

basis of the bitter and powerful humour of the
" Tale of a Tub," Carlyle catches up and com-
bines with an idealism which he learned from the
Germans, especially from Fichte, with a sentimental
humour which reminds us of Sterne and Richter,
and with a moral intensity which was his inborn
inheritance as a son of Calvinistic Scotland.   All
these elements are fused together by a restless
shaping imagination, which is not content till it has
turned every idea into a vivid and definite picture.
The result is one of the strangest, and in some
respects one of the most chaotic of books, a book
reducible to no recognised literary form ; but at
the same time a book rich in humour and imaginative insight, and full of that original force and
inspiring power, which belongs to the work of one
who insists on seeing and naming everything for
himself.   The main lesson which *Sartor Resartus*
seeks to teach is that, to the ordinary eye, this is
a world of deceiving and confusing shows and
appearances ; but that to the eye that can look
through the shows and penetrate to their deeper
meaning, it is a world of revelation, the manifestation of a spiritual principle.   " Matter," says
Carlyle, " were it never so despicable, is spirit, the
manifestation of spirit ; were it never so honour-
able, can it be more?"   " All visible things are
emblems ; what thou seest is not there on its own

account ; strictly taken, it is not there at all. Matter exists only spiritually and to represent some idea and body it forth.   Hence clothes, as despicable as we think them, are so unspeakably significant. Clothes, from the king's mantle downwards, are emblematic not of want only, but of a manifold coming victory over want.   On the other hand, all emblematic things are properly clothes, thought-woven or hand-woven.[1] " The universe itself is, as Goethe says, a 'living garment of deity,' a garment through which He reveals Himself to the eye of poet and prophet, and in a measure to every one who is prepared to see.   We sit as in a boundless phantasmagoria and dream-grotto : boundless, for the faintest star, the remotest century, lies not even nearer the verge thereof ; sounds and many coloured visions flit round our sense, but Him, the unslumbering, whose work both dream and dreamer are, we see not, except in rare half-waking moments, suspect not. ' Creation,' says one, lies before us like a glorious rainbow ; but the sun that made it lies behind us, hidden from us.'   Then in that strange dream how we clutch at shadows as if they were substances, and sleep deepest when fancying ourselves most awake!" [2]

If it be asked how this thesis is supported and

[1] Book I. Chap. XI.   [2] Book I. Chap. VIII.

developed in the *Sartor Resartus*, I must content myself here with two remarks on the *method* and the *matter* contained in it.

First, as to its *method*.   It is almost needless to say that you will not find in it an attempt to demonstrate anything logically, either by old or by new logical methods.   As to the former, Carlyle never loses an opportunity of, so to speak, insulting the syllogism and all the weapons of the old armoury of Logic.   And though he owes much to the later German philosophy, especially to Fichte's popular works, he seems to have cared only about the results, and nothing at all about the processes. Metaphysical theories in general, (though when he speaks in detail about them, we generally find him referring to the theories of the sensationalist and materialistic schools,) he regards as absurd attempts to measure the immensurable, or weigh with earthly scales that infinite reality, which we can, he thinks, imaginatively symbolise, but which we cannot scientifically define or determine.   Take one passage from many.   " Yes, friends," says Teufelsdröck, "not our logical, mensurative faculty, but our imaginative one, is king over us, priest and prophet to lead us heavenward, or magician and wizard to lead us hell-wards.   Nay, even for the basest sensualist, what is sense but the implement of phantasy, the vessel it drinks out of?

Even in the dullest existence there is a sheen either of inspiration or of madness, (thou partly hast it in thy choice which of the two,) that gleams in from the circumambient eternity, and colours with its own hues our little islet of time. The understanding indeed is thy window, too clear thou canst not make it, but phantasy is thy eye, with its colour-giving retina, healthy or diseased."[1] So also in the well-known essay entitled " Characteristics," Carlyle dwells on the fact that the absence of reflection and the presence of imaginative faith is that which distinguishes every healthy and noble period in the world's history, whereas it is the indication of a period of decay when men begin to reflect, to analyse, to philosophise.

I shall not trouble you at present with any vindication of philosophy, as I wish rather to use our time in making clear what exactly is Carlyle's view. And, indeed, the general idea of the sequence of an age of reflection upon an age of faith, upon which Carlyle insists, is a commonplace of modern philosophy, which he probably learned in the first instance from Fichte's lectures on the *Characteristics of the Present Age*. What is more to the purpose is to notice how Carlyle's conception of the power and work of imagination chimes in with the purpose of his book, which, as I have already

[1] Book III. Chap. III.

said, is to distinguish the reality from the show of phenomenon, which is its necessary manifestation. Viewing the universe as a mystery, in the sense that we cannot explain it, or find any speculative solution of its difficulties, he yet regards its inner meaning as an "open secret," which through manifold symbols reveals itself to the imaginative intuition of faith.   Hence, he is continually trying to enforce the lesson of what he calls " Natural Supernaturalism," by which he means that, whatever may be thought of special miracles, the whole world is miraculous. For what was a miracle supposed to be?   It was the indication that spirit is more and higher than matter.   But " natural supernaturalism " is the discovery that the natural world is itself the symbol, vesture, or phenomenon of a spiritual or divine power, which also manifests itself in a higher way in human history, as a divine justice which is always executing itself upon men and nations.   And here we find the key to one of what we may call Carlyle's paradoxes, " Speech is silvern, silence is golden."   By this he means that it is impossible, strictly speaking, to utter or fully express the truth.   You can only discover some more or less inadequate symbol for it, and your best symbol will lose its virtue if you do not make it a basis for action.   With regard to the first of these points, Carlyle seems to hold that, as it is impossible for us speculatively to explain the universe from its principle of unity, we can only set the truth before us and realise it for ourselves through some definite form of sense or imagination, which we take as a *symbol* to express the inexpressible. The history of religion is but the history of the different symbols which have successively risen into prominence and then worn themselves out to make way for better, or which, to use the fundamental metaphor of Carlyle, have been cast aside like old clothes, that humanity might re-invest itself in the garment of a new faith. But, again, such symbols, grasped by the intuitive imagination, have not, as Kant would have said, a speculative, but only a practical value. They have a kind of truth which we can test only by experiment on our own lives ; they embody beliefs upon which we can live, but which we cannot scientifically verify. Hence faith in them cannot be established by any purely speculative process. As Carlyle is fond of saying, " Doubt cannot be removed except by action." For the ancient precept " Know thyself," he would substitute " Know thy work." " Consider," he says, " how in the meanest kind of labour the whole soul of a man is composed to harmony as soon as he sets himself to work. Properly, thou hast no other knowledge but what thou hast got by working ; the rest is all a hypothesis of knowledge—a thing to be argued about in the schools—a thing floating in the clouds in endless logic vortices. Doubt of whatever kind can be ended by action alone."

The healthy state of man, then, is the state of unconscious, unreflective energy, in which his faith is like the air he breathes—something taken for granted, and made the basis of noble action.   Unhappily this is not always possible, for the best symbols gradually lose their power and become unbelievable, and there is always an interval of division, doubt, and weakness ere a new symbol can be created.   Now, it is our unhappy lot, according to Carlyle, to be born in a time when the old garments are worn out—a time of hesitation and doubt, in which the deeper meaning of the world has been lost.   " Two centuries ago," he declares, " they hung Cromwell's body from the Tigburn gallows, because he found the Christian religion inexcusable," and ever since men have attempted " to govern without God."   " Governing by the Christian law of God had been found a thing of battle, confusion, convulsion, an infinitely difficult thing," and it was resolved " to govern by only so much of God's Christian law as should prove quiet and convenient." [1]   From this time

[1] *Past and Present*, Book III. Chap. VI.

the decay of faith began, which has been gradually undermining our life, till we have now "pretty well exhausted what of firm earth there was for us to march on." Religion has become a hypocrisy, which has therefore called forth an atheistic philosophy to destroy it ; our poetry has become a mere plaything of idle moments, and our best singers sing " as from the throat outwards." " On the one side has been dreary cant, with a *reminiscence* of things holy and divine ; on the other side, acrid candour, with a *prophecy* of things brutal, infernal." Nature, instead of being to us a symbol and manifestation of the divine, has become for us a piece of dead mechanism ; and, what is worse than this, the mechanical view of things has extended itself to the life of man, which is now regarded by most simply as a machine, moved by the sensuous springs of pleasure and pain. With this, too, all idea of a social unity has been lost ; men have come to regard themselves as individual units, competing with each other, and trampling down each other in the struggle for material good. " *Laissez Faire* " is supposed to be the sole policy of government and " cash payment the sole nexus of man to man." And the inevitable result has followed— lawlessness and misery, anarchy and revolt.

This is what has come about, because the old

symbol of that reality which is higher than the
material or natural world has become worn out ;
no new accredited symbol has yet taken its place.
But the germs of a higher faith are already showing
themselves, and a more devout study of nature
and human history will develop them to maturity.
" Nature in late centuries was irreverently supposed to be dead, an old eight-day clock made
many thousand years ago, and still ticking on, but
as dead as brass, which the Maker at most sat
looking at, in a distant, singular, and now plainly
indeed, incredible manner. But now I am happy
to observe she is everywhere asserting herself not
to be dead brass at all, but alive and miraculous,
celestial-infernal, with an emphasis that will again
penetrate the thickest head on the planet by-and-
by." And with this consciousness of the life and
unity of nature, which is expressed above all in
Goethe's wonderful song of the " Earth Spirit,"
there is arising also a belief in a divine justice
which is not dead or sleeping, but revealing itself
to whoever has an eye to penetrate through the
superficial appearances, and discern the real meaning of human history. Might is right, for right
is the only real might. This inversion, which has
often been ill-interpreted, is but Carlyle's way of
expressing a faith that the apparent failure of good
is really victory. "Await the issue ; in all battles,

if you await the issue, each fighter is prospered according to his right. His right and his might, at the close of the account, were one and the same." " At the close of the account,"—Carlyle explains what he means by this in the immediately following words, " He has fought with all his might, and in exact proportion to his right he has prevailed. His very death is no victory over him ; he dies, indeed, but his work lives. The cause thou fightest for, so far as it is true, no further, but precisely so far, is sure of victory."

What shall we say of this creed? We might call it, in Carlyle's own language, a Christianity divested of almost all its clothing ; a Christianity without supernaturalism, without dogmas, and without church, reduced to the belief that the universe is in its deepest meaning spiritual, and that therefore, as he expresses it, " the true Shekinah is man " ; a belief, in other words, that in the moral life of man we have the clearest revelation or symbol of that which the divine Spirit is. The new element which makes Carlyle's re- statement of this faith more than a spectre of abstraction derived from Christianity is that which it has in common with the German idealism, namely, the attempt to show, not that spirit interferes with matter, or miraculously works upon it from without, but that the material or sensible world is *itself*, in its deepest essence, spiritual. Thus, beneath and beyond the phenomena of outward nature there is a reality unknown to science, because the methods and categories of science are inadequate to reach it, but revealed in that highest kind of poetry which is truth. And, again, in human history, when we have exhausted all the ordinary casual explanation of events, we have still to leave room for an ultimate interpretation of them by that moral necessity, according to which, in the words of Schiller, " *Die Welt-Geschichte ist das Welt-Gericht*," the history of the world is the judgment of the world. This doctrine Carlyle does not, as I have already said, seek to prove in any logical or philosophical way ; he rather seeks, if one may use a somewhat inadequate word, to *illustrate* it. In other words, he seeks to show in case after case how, before the penetrative power of imaginative insight, the facts of nature and history become transparent and disclose their deeper meaning.

Of the outward nature, indeed, Carlyle speaks only in the way of casual remark, though he is always seeking out analogies, which tend to show that the ultimate meaning of the natural is the spiritual. But the aim of all his great historical works is, in Milton's phrase, " to vindicate the ways of God to man." He has too much faith to wish to twist the facts of history, or to feel any need to twist them, in order to point a moral.

His accuracy in relation to all the local and personal detail of his story is unimpeachable, and, indeed, rises to a level very rarely attained even by the most exact of modern historians. But he is always trying to penetrate beneath the facts to the ultimate moral forces, upon the strength of which he believes the conflict to turn, and to show that, in spite of all appearance to the contrary, the soul of the world is just. And the great weapon which he uses to attain this result is his strange gift of combined humour and imagination —a gift which enables him, in painting the events of history, continually to keep before us at once the greatness and the littleness of men, the narrowness and finitude of the interests for which they contend, when we regard these interests in themselves, and their infinite importance when we look at their moral significance.

Thus, he never fails to project his pictures, as it were, upon a background of the infinite ; and to show at once the absurdity and the pathos of the doings of men when they are contemplated " *sub specie æternitatis.*" Nor does he ever fail to point the moral that, viewed in this highest light, all the importance which is bestowed upon events and persons, by any accidental or outward cause, disappears, till they are lowered or exalted to their true place, as the manifestation of spiritual forces. He tries, in short, to make us see through the external puppet-show of human life, to the internecine struggle of good and evil which is half reveals and half conceals.

And his great power of doing this enables us to understand another of what I have called Carlyle's paradoxes, the doctrine, namely, that poets, at least in the present age, should cease to sing, or, as he puts it, that they should cease to "invent anything but reality." By this he means that they should henceforth cease to produce what is called fiction, and should confine themselves to the task of throwing the light of their imagination upon history and biography. Carlyle even goes so far in this direction as to regret that Shakespeare gave so much of his faculty to fresh constructive efforts, and so little to the illumination of the history of England. "And yet of Shakespeare, too," he declares, "it is not the fiction I admire, but the fact. To say truth, what I most of all admire are the traces he shows of a talent that could have turned the history of England into a kind of *Iliad*, almost, perhaps, into a kind of *Bible*."

To controvert such a literary heresy as this is unnecessary. It is enough to say, from Carlyle's

own point of view, that truth and the detail of
accident and circumstance are not the same thing,
and that the attempt to hold to the latter with
exactness can rarely be coincident with the highest
expression of the former.   Is it in *Richard the
Third* and *Henry the Fifth*, or in *Lear* and
Hamlet, that Shakespeare gives us the deepest
truth?   Carlyle's great faculty of penetrative insight, his power of seeing the poetry of life
through the most ordinary details, and, we must
add, his want of the highest power, either of
abstract thinking on the one side or of creative
imagination on the other, produced in him a kind
of intolerance of every form of literary utterance
except that in which he himself was strongest.
We might even say that in insisting upon the
importance of fact, he sometimes confused the
sense of the word in which he uses it, when he says
that " the infinite is most sure of all facts," with
the sense in which it is a fact that we had several
meals yesterday.   As usual, however, his paradox
is but the one-sided expression of a truth,—the
truth, namely, that the only ideas worth attending
to are those which have been and are realising
themselves in the world, even through the very
appearances or " facts " that seem to obstruct
them ; and that the very highest value of literature, whether poetical, historical, or philosophical,

is to open our eyes to these ideals. Such an explanation enables us to be just to Carlyle, and at the same time to escape from the conclusions to which he would lead us.

I have not left myself room to say almost anything of Carlyle's practical application of his principles to the political and social life of his time, but I must add a few words on this topic. All his writings on such questions—*Past and Present, Chartism,* etc.—are closely related to his great historical works. The theme which he tries to illustrate in both is the decay and the renewal of belief, and therefore of the social order that is dependent upon it. In his *French Revolution* he paints the great conflagration that resulted from the decay of the old social order of France. In the lives of Cromwell and Frederic he shows us how, by the influence of a heroic personality, the life and unity of a nation may be restored ; and in his political pamphlets I need scarcely say that his one great fundamental idea is *Hero-worship*. He cares little or nothing for forms of government, and regards them all as simply means to find the true hero and put him in his rightful place. " Hero-worship," he asserts, " done differently in every different epoch of the world, is the soul of all social business among men ; the doing of it ill, or the doing of it well, measures exactly what degree of well-being or of ill-being there is in the world's affairs." [1]

He recognises indeed, at least in his earlier works, that the methods of modern hero-worship, or of getting our real captains, will be different from those of earlier times, and even that they involve in a greater degree the consent of the governed. If he declares that "an actual new Sovereignty, Industrial Aristocracy—real, not imaginary aristocracy—is indispensable for us," and that a state of society in which there is no nexus of man to man but cash payment cannot last, he yet acknowledges that "we are to bethink us that men cannot now be bound to men by *brass collars*" (as Gurth, the swine-herd, was in *Ivanhoe*). "Not at all — that brass-collar method, in all figures of it, has vanished out of Europe for evermore. Huge Democracy, walking the streets everywhere in its sack coat, has asserted so much, irrevocably, brooking no reply." He even adds that the true question for the modern time is, "How in conjunction with inevitable Democracy indispensable Sovereignty is to exist." [2] But he always admits so much with a kind of grudge, and in his later works he seems to recoil from the admission, and to regard the advance toward

[1] *Past and Present*, Book I. Chap. VI.
[2] *Past and Present*, Book IV. Chap. I.

Democracy as a mere " Shooting Niagara." He cannot believe that, under a democratic system, the real leaders of men will get to the front, and he has no belief whatever in any tendency of a free nation to work its way by freedom to the correction of its own errors. His greatest aberration, his defence of slavery, and the astonishing blunder—for we can count it no less in a man like him—that made him altogether blind to the real meaning of the American War, are connected with this. We are told, however, by Mr. Froude that he afterwards acknowledged that there was perhaps more in that great struggle than he had discerned at the time.

The truth is that Carlyle was strongly individualistic in his whole tone of mind. He had, at least, no firm grasp of the organic unity or *solidarity* of human life, or of the creative powers of those social forces which arise, not from the individuals taken separately, but from the way in which they act and react upon each other in society. In his own life he stood apart from other men, confident in himself and his judgments ; and though penetrating in his insight into character, yet he was quite incapable of the " give and take " of social life, or, indeed, of doing anything in regard to others, except simply to insist on his own will and his own opinions. It was in harmony with this that, in his view of history, he had his eye fixed mainly on the doings of certain leaders, and far too little on the general stream of thought and life which carried both leaders and followers along with it. In this point of view the very title of Emerson's book, *Representative Men*, is a kind of silent criticism upon Carlyle's *Heroes and Hero-worship*. In social politics, again, Carlyle had far too high an estimate of the advantage of men being *driven* into the right road, and far too low an estimate of the difference between that method and the method of governing them through their own will.

At the same time, every one must admit that Carlyle is right in saying that the success of this, as of every system, must depend greatly on the ability of men to recognise and to reverence those who are their true guides and superiors, though such reverence need by no means imply anything like an absolute submission, either of opinion or will. But Carlyle, whom we may call the modern Elijah, was ever too apt, like the ancient Elijah, to think that he was standing alone, and above all others required to be told that there were yet seven thousand men in Israel who had not bowed the knee to Baal. And as in his picture of history he was apt to become almost a special pleader for the individual he had selected as hero, so in politics he was inclined to regard all responsibility of the rulers to the people as a hindrance to the efficient ruling of the hero when he should be found.   On the other hand, our view of his political thought would not be complete without noting how much he did to banish the eighteenth-century theory of the limitations of the government to the functions of a grand policeman, and to revive the old Platonic idea that the State had a social and ethical work to perform — an idea which, it may be remarked, could scarcely be realised in modern times by any Government without a strong democratic force behind it.

With these insufficient words I must leave Carlyle's political pamphlets.   Their great power lies, not in the specific proposals which they contain, or even in the truth of their analysis of the political situation, but in their constant preaching of the lesson that a moral regeneration of society is more important than any change of the machinery of government, and is indeed necessary to make any such change effective.   They lift us out of the atmosphere of party, and force us to look beyond special measures to the deepest social problems ; and they are full of words of reproof, of warning, and encouragement, winged with insight, humour, and imagination, which thrill through us like battle music.   After everything has been said that can be said in the way of criticism, we are forced to recognise that no English writer in this century has done more to elevate and purify our ideals of life, and to make us conscious that the things of the spirit are real, and that, in the last resort, there is no other reality.

INDEX

INDEX